How I Became a Tree

How
I Became a
Tree

. . . . .

SUMANA ROY

Yale
UNIVERSITY
PRESS
New Haven & London

First published in India in 2017 by Aleph Book
Company.
First published in the United States and the
United Kingdom by Yale University Press in 2021.

Yale University Press books may be purchased in
quantity for educational, business, or promotional use.
For information, please e-mail sales.press@yale.edu
(U.S. office) or sales@yaleup.co.uk (U.K. office).

Text design by Bena Sareen, copyright © Aleph Book
Company 2017.

Printed in the United States of America.

Library of Congress Control Number: 2021936463
ISBN 978-0-300-26044-1 (hardcover : alk. paper)
ISBN 978-0-300-26814-0 (paperback)

A catalogue record for this book is available from the
British Library.

10 9 8 7 6 5 4 3 2 1

Not that I want to be a god or a hero.
Just to change into a tree, grow for ages, not hurt anyone.
—Czesław Miłosz

CONTENTS

Part I

A Tree Grew inside My Head
—Octavio Paz, *A Tree Within*

TREE TIME

At first it was the underwear. I wanted to become a tree because trees did not wear bras.

Then it had to do with the spectre of violence. I loved the way in which trees coped with dark and lonely places while sunlessness decided curfew hours for me. I liked too how trees thrived on things that were still freely available—water, air and sunlight; and no mortgage in spite of their lifelong occupation of land.

My amorphous fancies about trees began to coalesce when I entered middle age and began to weigh the benefits of a freelancer's life against that of a salaried professional. An epiphany wrapped me like a tendril—were trees freelancers or salaried employees? A tree was a daily wage labourer, its life of work bound to the cycle of sunlight. Holidays, vacations, weekends, the salaried life, pension, loans—all of these were recent inventions, nothing more than consolations offered to employees like myself.

So, when I look back at the reasons for my disaffection with being human, and my desire to become a tree, I can see that at root lay the feeling that I was being bulldozed by time. As I removed my watch from my wrist, and clocks from my walls, I realized that all my flaws—and this I now discover I share with many others—came from my failure to be a good slave to time. I began envying the tree, its disobedience to human time. All around me were estate developers sending their fleets of workers to construct skyscrapers to tight schedules. The trees they planted in the gated communities annoyed them—they would grow at their natural pace. It was impossible to rush plants, to tell a tree to 'hurry up'. In envy, in admiration and with ambition, I began to call that pace 'Tree Time'. (Was it this that Salvador Dalí wanted to invoke when he placed so many of his melting clocks on trees in his paintings?)

I was tired of speed. I wanted to live to tree time. This I felt most excruciatingly during examination hall invigilation, while keeping guard over the exhausted faces of my students, their having to condense a year into a few hours, the learning acquired at different times of the day and in different places cramped into a few hours of writing time. That was how one passed examinations, got degrees and jobs, measured success. A tree did not stay up all night to become a successful examinee the next morning. Plant life, in spite of its various genres of seasonal flowers and fruits, did not—could not—do that. One can't tinker with the timing of a yawn, one cannot play with tree time.

I began by abandoning newspapers, news television and news suppliers. These capsules of heightened and condensed time had come to divide our attention, splintered our life into bullets. Plants were not newsmakers because they could not cause coups or wars. Plants were not news consumers because their world remained unaffected by changes in governments and results of cricket matches. Apart from the weather—not its forecast, mind you, that comedy show on television—the plant world was indifferent to every occurrence, man-made or natural, outside the locality of its amphitheatre. The day's work anaesthetized me, left me incompetent to deal with humans, their order and orders. Talk, the incessant word-by-word relay of the goings-on, always and inevitably of humans, on the earth, in the air, under water, generated a claustrophobia in me that is difficult to explain—I am daughter to a man who is a news junkie, who watches the same piece of news on the state-sponsored Doordarshan channel in Bangla, Hindi and then Urdu. I found myself in a world where being a repository of news—as telegrams—turned one into a sort of activist. And all the news that mattered was, of course, almost exclusively, bad news. This timbre of nervous energy that had turned the world into an apocalypse movie was the resident spirit of the newsroom—we were all doomed, all moving towards a terrifying end, we were all a part of the news.

Sumana Roy

The newspaper was the new holy book and the news reader the new priest. The unnatural rhythm of news, the panting pace at which it now moved, caused me breathlessness. I wanted to move out, out of this news as neighbourhood. And so my attraction to the tree and its complete indifference to the hypnosis of news.

Once upon a time, I was certain, men and trees moved to the same rhythm, lived their lives to the same time. To gain an understanding of this concept that, of course, existed only in my imagination, I began planting saplings to mark births and beginnings. When my nephew was born five years ago, for instance, I planted a neem tree in our backyard. The little boy stands at three feet or so. The neem tree is taller than my husband who is six feet tall. But before this was the tree that is as old as my marriage. I did not plant it. The municipal corporation did, as part of its city greening project. It was just a happy happenstance, then, that the gulmohar tree with its yellow flowers came to be planted a few days before my wedding, and that too, just opposite the room from where my married life would begin. It is now taller than our three-storeyed house, and it allows me to imagine an alternative version of my marriage as a tree, a life I might have lived had I allowed myself to live to tree time.

Allied to human notions of time is an overwhelming ageism. People have often told me—I refrain from using the word 'compliment' because I cannot think of 'youthful looks' as praise—that I looked young for my age. I found the words offensive and discriminatory: wasn't every division of age—old, middle, the many varieties that came as prefix and critique—beautiful? One morning, when I received such a 'compliment', I couldn't help wondering how a tree might have reacted. If I was a forty-year-old tree, would I not have felt insulted to be considered twenty on the basis of my appearance? Age, I was certain, was important to trees. The wrinkles on our face and neck, the accumulation of folds around hips and thighs had, civilizationally, become embarrassing to humans. The age of trees was to be found in similar lines, in circles denoting lived years, in the girth of time that gave aged trees a kind of sober dignity. By looking at trees one could see that time was an obese creature. And that history, whether it was reflected in lines or folds, loose bark or skin, new colours or pigmentation, was a beautiful thing. Our lives in the industrial age, lived bizarrely as an approximation of machines, had made us think of age as ugly—in the way machines rusted, wasted, and gradually became ugly before they fell apart.

But how does one live to tree time in this deadlined world? I began by trying to dismantle the architecture of time units inside my head. It wasn't completely a conscious effort, but the whole manner of our timekeeping begins to look silly when one asks a tree the question that inaugurates application forms and conversations: 'When is your birthday?' I had taken off information about my birthday from Facebook, for instance. I felt awkward when people asked me about my birth date. I also couldn't understand why our culture, both social and bureaucratic, placed such great emphasis on the date of our arrival into the world. I knew no one who celebrated the birthdays of trees. I also found it difficult to picture trees celebrating death anniversaries. Wedding anniversaries would be a joke given the number of 'marriages' a tree went through in its lifespan. What exactly was 'tree time' then? I wandered aimlessly through philosophical discussions on time until it came to me one night, in my salty sleep: carpe diem, seize the moment, living in the present—that was tree time, a life without worries for the future or regret for the past. There's sunlight: gulp, swallow, eat, there's night: rest. And I began writing this to tree time, recording thoughts as they arrived, events as they occurred, and fighting insomnia and its derivative poetry like a good tree.

WOMEN AS FLOWERS

Centuries of conditioning, of literature and artwork that have entered the stream of the colloquial have enforced the visual equivalence between women and flowers. It seems 'natural' to name a woman after a flower—nature is, we are never allowed to forget, prakriti, a woman. At first, it comes from grandma's tales. In 'Ghumonto Puri', the second story of *Thakurmar Jhuli*, a collection of grandmother's tales in Bangla, for instance, a young prince sets out on a 'desh-bhromon'—he will travel through his kingdom to find out more about its beauty and its people. Travelling alone, without a companion or bodyguard, with only a new sword, he continues walking across mountains and through rivers until he reaches a forest. But it is unlike any forest he has seen— there are no bird or animal cries here, and when he enters its depths he discovers a kingdom. There are sky-kissing mansions and palaces, soldiers and their arsenal of warfare, beautiful citizens, the king on his throne, the ministers in their court, gold and precious gems in the treasury, but there is not a single drop of sound in the kingdom. Everything and everyone is frozen in time, there is no movement anywhere, and so no leaf falls from trees.

Amidst this statuesque forest, where the air is heavy with stillness and nothing moves, the young prince suddenly becomes aware of the fragrance of flowers. The fragrance of a thousand blooming lotuses is the only thing that has moved ever since he came here. When he enters the flower garden, directed by the fragrance, he finds a bed made of gold and embossed with diamonds, and hanging from them numerous flower garlands, and amidst gold lotuses, a beautiful princess poisoned with sleep. The prince falls in love and spends years waiting for her to wake up from her sleep until one day he discovers a golden stick that performs that function. When she awakens, things in the kingdom begin to move and statues regain their form to become men and trees and fruits and flowers.

Two things in particular stand out in my reading of the tale: the deathly quiet of a world where nothing moves; and the stifling passivity of the girl. That movement should be equated with life is a kind of notion that is terribly exclusionary—it is the reason the old and the ailing are so easily dismissed with the cruel adjective 'lifeless'. In the same group falls plant life—botanists and philosophers have, for centuries, considered plants inferior to animals (anima; animate, the same root) because they do not 'move'. But plants do move, a fact earthworms, they of supposedly inferior intelligence, have always known better than humans.

In this imagined death-world, it is a bit of a contradiction then to find that what moves to bring the story to a happy climax must emanate from a tree: the fragrance of flowers. Sleep seems to be the closest approximation of death, an abbreviated death as it were, and it strikes me as odd that the prince should fall in love with the sleeping princess's beauty. Yes, all mothers of crying infants would think of sleep, both theirs and their sleeping babies, as the most beautiful thing in the world, but what is it about a sleeping princess that makes her beautiful?

The princess, covered and protected and nurtured by fragrant flowers, *is* a flower for all purposes. Beauty, fragrance, colour, softness, the ease with which it can be plucked, displaced from plant to vase, an object of decoration and much else—all these together have turned the woman into a flower in the male gaze. But what pleases men most in this analogy is the passivity of the flower and the woman. Mary Beard, in her fine essay 'The Public Voice of Women', has most forcefully argued that our writers and philosophers have privileged the dumb (in both senses—one who does not speak as much as men do, and one who does not possess intelligence comparable to a man's) woman over the thinking, argumentative woman. Passivity must therefore be the woman's ultimate seduction ploy. In this equivalence, the tree or plant is the patriarch; leaves, because they work all day for food, the male labourer; flowers the stay-at-home beneficiaries of that labour; and fruits, of course, the necessary consequence of such an alliance.

Bengali girls are often named after flowers—my neighbourhood was full of girls whose names made them relatives of flowers. Golap and Golapi, the rose; Jui, a variety of jasmine; Padma, the lotus; Dopati, balsam; Shiuli and Shefali, the coral jasmine and the night-flowering jasmine; Madhobilata, Parijat, Henna; Chandramallika, the chrysanthemum; the sweet smelling Beli and Rajnigandha; also the English names Dahlia, Zinnia, Jasmine, even Rose. But I do not know anyone whose name is 'gachh' or tree. It is unfair, this prejudice, of favouring the beauty of flowers over the trees that produce it. I have considered it, standing in a queue in a district court, a piece of stamped paper in hand, to get an affidavit that would allow me to legally use Gachh as my surname.

From a very young age, I was made conscious of the fact that I was not a flower. I had neither its beauty nor delicacy. My mother had passed on her beauty to my brother, I heard our relatives mourn for me from time to time. When I was old enough to play Match-the-Column, comparing myself with my parents, I found that I had possibly only inherited my father's enthusiasm for the non-serious and his proclivity for questioning every piece of received wisdom. Both these traits are useless to a child, and so in primary school I watched with a child's envy and sense of deprivation, at school functions, prettier classmates getting their lips and cheeks painted, being given headgear resembling the yellow petals of a sunflower. I would be the tree, a green cardboard mop for a head—even at that age, when none of the teachers cared to apply makeup to my face, I knew that the beauty of flowers lay in close-ups, of specificities, while trees were far more generic in our consciousness. Of course I did not have the wherewithal to articulate my self-pity then, but drawing class had taught me that when I painted colours on flowers, someone would inevitably ask what flower it was, but unless I drew a coconut tree with needle like pencil marks or pine trees that looked like sliced staircases, no one bothered with the names of trees in children's drawing books.

The awareness of that lack would define and mould my

relationships with other humans and trees, but as a teenager, when I would find the words to articulate my sense of deprivation to my father, he, never one to lose his side of the argument, would say, 'But you are a flower. Ask your Hindi teacher. What does "suman" mean, after all?' 'Suman' is the Hindi word for 'flower', a generic flower. My Hindi-speaking friends have, for most of my life, called me 'Suman' and not 'Sumana'. It did not take me long to realize my father's half-truth—'Sumana' is a synthesis of 'su' and 'mana', meaning 'good' and 'mind' respectively and while I was happy to have a 'good mind', it was all too clear to me that it was the female face that was compared to a flower. After all, no man had ever marvelled at the intelligence of a human mind and called it a flower.

So why was I so keen on becoming a tree? And was my malady exclusive to me alone?

I gradually began to grow aware of my body's participation in this enterprise. I had never been a makeup person—a kohl pencil and tinted lip balm were the only coloured things I had occasionally used on my face. Kohl for my soul, I often told myself, as I dragged the eye pencil towards the outer edges of my eyes, giving them boundaries for the day. Sometimes it felt that if I didn't, the pupils would fall out of the socket. Such imaginings.

But I didn't know a single tree which needed to use makeup. These moments of self-recognition began to come in installments. I remember it coming to me at the hairdresser's once as I sat on the raised stool and the talkative woman sprayed water onto my hair and then gave it a trim. In the mirrors in front and behind me, I watched her focused gaze, and it suddenly reminded me of the look on our gardener's face as he trimmed shrubs and fast-growing plants against my wish. Both the hairdresser and the gardener seemed to believe in the value of snips and cuts for a better future, and in this I began to see the kinship of my undisciplined hair with the wayward branches of trees. I had begun to *feel* the violence of seasonal pruning and cutting that was inflicted on plants and trees. Parks became parlours and gardens beauty salons in my mind. And so I now find myself unable to wear earrings—I have the sensation of someone hammering a nail through tight tree bark. There is also the epidemic of fairness: skin-whitening agents live inside most cosmetic creams in India, promising protection from sunlight. Sunscreens have turned the sun into the likeness of a torturer, someone spraying dark tans on otherwise perfect canvasses. I had managed to avoid sunscreens all my life—their shininess resembled the Indian wrestler's oiled skin to me, something that turned the sun into a tormentor. It only needed my plants on the window to tell me like it really was—through the iron grille their thin stems and small leaves had all turned away from me, their water-giver, towards the sun's face. Sunlight was their food—they had opened themselves to it like beggars open their hands for alms. In front of me, then, was an illustration of why some ancient civilizations had worshipped the sun as god. And in it was a critique of man's recent rejection of sunlight on skin. My window plants left me with another aphoristic thought—that branches and leaves of a tree seek the sun with as much curious energy as its roots reach out for water. Was this movement in opposite directions—northwards for the sun and southwards for water—a natural bipolarity that psychologists had, after all the head-heart romanticized allegories, called bipolar disorder in humans?

I tried to avoid turning tree life into parables like these, but they rose to the surface from time to time, especially when I began to think about living like a tree. This happened, I can confess now, when I saw the epidemic of abundance around me. Ours was an age of excess—more food and clothes and houses and things than we needed, an extravagant show of wealth and emotions without either being connected to the inner life. I liked what I thought was the restraint in plants. It wasn't actually restraint but a natural order that we like to call balance. There was no gluttony, no anorexia—plants ate only as much as they needed, and so they suffered neither from obesity nor malnutrition. In plant economics, need and want are one and the same thing, unlike in the human world where wants had the character of a capitalist bulldozer whose actions could be justified through the prettified word 'desire'. And so there was no envy, the by-product of this gap between I-want and She-has-it. I looked at neighbouring trees, sometimes at the canopies that they formed overhead, and inspected them naively for traces of the violence of greed and jealousy. Who has ever seen a tree and exclaimed, 'Such a jealous tree!', the way we do about children in the playground and adults in an auction hall? I wanted that confidence of the tree, the complete rejection of all that made humans feel inferior or superior. (No one has ever thought of grass suffering from an inferiority complex, after all, I reminded myself in an aside.)

The other kind of weariness that came over me at this time had to do with the exhibition of 'relationship status'. This seemed to matter to everyone: the curious inspection of fingers for the engagement ring, strangers looking for vermilion in the parting of a Hindu woman's hair, the hotel receptionist asking to put a 'Mrs' before my name in the register, the law asking for marital status on every form. This valorization of one relationship as the central axis around which one's life must move, this exclusively human prejudice, had been turned into an epidemic. I belonged to the majority group that had been happily colonized by it despite the fact that I wore no signs of my relationship with my husband. I had worn no sign of my status as offspring or sibling, why would I wear it as a spouse? Trees wore no relationship uniform, one could not look at a tree and declare whether it was happily married or that it had got recently divorced, whether it was a widow or single. I longed to become this, liberated of identity tags.

And this naturally led to my thinking about love. The word is common currency now: polyamory, loving more than one person; romantic love, that is. I wondered why it was the norm in our largely monogamous culture to be married to only one person, whereas it was all right to love more than one plant or tree. But there was also something else. The Germanic root for 'truth'—as also 'trust'—derives from the firmness and steadfastness of a tree. Glenn W. Erickson, in *The Philosophy of Forestry*, writes about this being the reason for marriage vows being taken under a bower, so that 'the one who commits himself will be as strong and straight as the oak or the ash, the birch or the beech, in whose presence the ritual is enacted'.

Was I being adulterous in loving more than one tree?

THE KINDNESS OF PLANTS

From an air-shut room in the cruellest days of winter, I watched Buddhist prayer flags move to the moods of the wind. A tiny burst of cold wind could set me coughing for long minutes—my room, with its shut windows, its valve-like sternness, was all I had during those weeks, sometimes months, of affliction. There were many potted plants in our bedroom. One by one, I had them moved out onto the adjacent balcony and the large sills of our French windows: my bouts of asthmatic breathlessness had made me acutely sensitive to the needs of my fellow beings. The feeling of my plants being asphyxiated left me out of breath. Watching the tall and colourful prayer flags on the neighbour's terrace was the closest I got to experience the play of wintry winds. From my bed, where weakness and exhaustion had chained me, I gradually got used to a different perspective of my world, and certainly my life. The notion of 'eye level' or 'eye contact' changed—being in bed turned the ceiling into an ally. I could make out the time of the day from the angles at which shadows of the world outside played on its surface. Most often these were shadows of coconut and betel nut trees from the neighbour's backyard. The palm leaves sneaked into my room as shadows—I watched and gauged the fierceness of the wind from their sway and swing on the white ceiling. I envied them their immunity to what Bengalis call 'season change'—as if the weather were a disease. Anti-allergy medicines kept me in bed for ten hours—sleep seemed to me, at times, like a great preservative that would protect me from disease and death. Freedom must be a great preservative too, and I wondered whether it was that, the freedom from an illness that made the horizontal position the default one that kept trees largely disease-neutral. It was perhaps also this freedom that made me long to be a tree.

᭥

Kindness, I had been told by friends and therapists, was my hamartia, my fatal flaw. Were plants kind creatures? The moral biology of junior-school science teaches us to think of plants as altruistic creatures, who kindly gave us our oxygen and fruits and flowers and vegetables and shade and support for swings. But this was to be my lesson—if I really wanted to become a tree, I would need to rev up my consciousness about self-love. The care of the self is a complicated concept, and I would never be sure if the French philosopher Michel Foucault meant to include trees in its fold. The Bengali idiom that came to me most often, from family no less, that unit which is usually most critical, was this: 'awpatray daan', I was putting my alms in the wrong bowl is what I was told.

So, are trees kind? Was it possible that the moral ecologists had got it all wrong, that trees were not really kind to others? That they survived only on self-interest? Biology tells us this, and yet men have turned trees into symbols of altruism. I was not interested in the quarrel between the two schools of thought. I was only curious to know whether trees too did what I had been accused of doing—donating alms to the wrong person? A tree, because it does not—cannot—know the difference between a gardener and a woodcutter, would treat both equally and not keep its breath of oxygen, flower, fruit and fragrance from either. In refusing to make this moral distinction, the tree would cause itself harm the way I probably did. But there was no way the tree could change. How could I then?

Like most people of my social class and education, I like to flatter and indulge myself with illusions about my infinite reserves of tolerance. Like many others like me, I have seen the violence of intolerance destroying relationships; what it does to communities and countries is on the first pages of newspapers. Because of my disillusionment with the noise of this human intolerance, or perhaps because of my own intolerance of this intolerance, an acute lack in my estimate, I began to wonder whether the idea of tolerance played out in the plant world. Free association with this concept brought with it other grudges that stoked my desire to flee to a plant life. I felt repulsed by the mechanics of human historiography—think of the way in which a man's quiet, possibly self-contented days are dismissed with a phrase like 'an uneventful life'. Literature too, especially the novel, in mimicking history, had privileged a false notion of time and busyness, a fact that was brought home to me particularly when I was working on my doctoral dissertation on the writer and musician Amit Chaudhuri, whose writing derives so much of its beauty from an aesthetic in which, in Samuel Beckett's half-jocular words, 'nothing happens'. Our dismissal of plant life comes from our inability to engage with nothing happening, with the Heraclitean 'nature loves to hide'.

Twentieth-century historians had tried to correct that impulse by bringing those whom they considered the 'marginalized' into the frame of history. But they hadn't been entirely able to escape from the domination of the 'event' on history. Only those who had caused abrupt roadblocks in the onward notion of time and event had made their way into history books. But there was nothing climactic, path-bending or life-changing in the life history of plants and trees. And hence their banishment from history? A neo-scientific colloquial phrase had been invented to trap the varied histories of all kinds of plant life—'life cycle' was drab compared to all the colourful and even artistic terminology reserved for humans. Plants and trees had therefore not *made* history. There was no record of plant behaviour apart from the bureaucratic note-taking of committed botanists.

Part of the reason behind this had to do with the privileging of creatures with eyes over those that didn't have them. The dominance of the visual in our lives, the way we lived, ate, dressed, spoke, sneezed, coughed, walked, ran, laughed, cried, was exasperating. History, thus, had only been about the visible. History textbooks are filled with stories of conquests because war results in graphic images. Or to relate what I am talking about to the everyday—a broken leg gets an employee medical leave but not a broken heart. It is this lopsided attitude that has made us indifferent to the invisible workings of plant life—we only see new leaves and flowers and fruits and make conclusions about a tree's health, everything else being inconsequential to us. And so the stress on the 'secret' in the titles of books that aim to tell us about their inner lives—the secret life of plants, the secret life of seeds, and so on. Secrets have never been given space or even footnoted in any history book, and so plants continue to remain ahistorical creatures.

But, of course, this is not about the visual element alone. It also has to do with movement. Take the circus, for instance, where animals and acrobats are put on show to display movements as evidence of the grand definition of life. Who has ever seen a tree or a plant in a circus? This explains their exclusion from the genre of children's toys; and adult 'toys' as well. Sometimes, leaning against a tree, I think of the Leaning Tower of Pisa and wonder why that piece of human architecture has been valorized while trees, with their extraordinary ability to grow in all kinds of directions, horizontal, vertical, and all manner of odd angles and hybrid postures in between, have been ignored.

I was often chastised for my madness. This love, this juvenile desire to live like a tree, was escapism, I was told, from a world of human cruelty and bloodshed. Bertolt Brecht wrote, 'You can't write poems about trees when the woods are full of policemen.'

But I was unfazed by the criticism. I was tired of the world I lived in, with all the tricks and subterfuges that were necessary to succeed. Trees were not politically correct—apart from the stratagems to attract possible pollinators, they did not need to engage in any kind of camouflage; there was no gap between who they were and who they wanted to be.

Tired of making mistakes, I turned to the plant world for lessons. Where was the scope of making mistakes in the emotional economy of a tree's life? 'It has been said that trees are imperfect men, and seem to bemoan their imprisonment rooted in the ground. But they never seem so to me. I never saw a discontented tree,' wrote John Muir in 1890. That is what I wanted to be.

Sumana Roy

THE WOMAN AS TREE

That I was not the first person to think of a woman as a tree was a relief. D. H. Lawrence helped me look at my body as a tree—his poem, 'Figs', liberated my breasts and vagina from their femaleness.

> The fig is a very secretive fruit.
> As you see it standing growing, you feel at once it is symbolic:
> And it seems male.
> But when you come to know it better, you agree with the
> Romans, it is female.
>
> The Italians vulgarly say, it stands for the female part; the fig-
> fruit:
> The fissure, the yoni,
> The wonderful moist conductivity towards the centre...

Every fruit has its secret.
   …That's how it should be, the female should always be a secret.
   The tree-as-woman genre of art is now almost a cliché, but a few striking paintings continue to stay with me. Anil Karanjai, in a Hungry Generation painting from the 1990s, draws a forest—inside it is a clearing, resembling a woman's vagina. There's Salvador Dalí's *The Tree Woman*, a female body branched like a tree, and the *Woman with a Head of Roses*; there's also Frida Kahlo, she who said 'I paint flowers so they will not die', imagining herself as a tree in her paintings— her face, a self-portrait, surrounded by sunflower petals in *Self-Portrait Inside a Sunflower*.
   Banaphool, the pseudonym of the Bengali writer Balai Chand Mukhopadhyay, that name meaning 'flowers of the forest' holding in

it an ambition similar to mine, has a story titled 'The Tree'. It's an old favourite, and it is completely different in character from other woman-as-tree imaginings because it does not have the dreaminess of liberation that I romantically associate with turning into a tree. The tree's bark was boiled, its leaves ground into a paste or fried or munched, its twigs used to clean teeth, all of these for medicinal purposes. Everyone was pleased with it, but no one actually cared for it.

> Suddenly, a different sort of person came up to it one day.
> He gazed, enraptured, at the tree. He didn't peel off its bark, didn't pluck its leaves, didn't snap its wings. Only looked on, captivated.
> 'How beautiful these leaves are,' he said. 'How lovely their lines. How pretty these clumps of flowers—a constellation of stars has descended from the blue skies to this green space...Wonderful...'
> Having gazed to his heart's content, he left.
> He was a man in search of a muse, not medicine.
> The neem tree wanted to run away with him. But it couldn't. Its roots had dug too deep into the earth. It stood behind the house in a heap of garbage.
> In that house, the housewife, so adept at domestic chores, was in the same situation.

I know that I want to be neither—not muse, not medicine. Why did I want to be a tree then?

༈

But I was not alone. Annette Giesecke, talking about Ovid's *Metamorphoses* in her book *The Mythology of Plants: Botanical Lore from Ancient Greece and Rome* writes: 'The reader encounters a vast, seemingly eclectic assemblage of Greek and Roman myths tenuously united only by the motif of transformation, generally of a human or divine being into an animal or plant.' I discovered a grandparent in Ovid.

Take the 'story' of Daphne, for instance. Apollo fell in love with Daphne, Peneus's daughter—Apollo had taunted Cupid for playing around with a bow and arrow, and Cupid, to take revenge, took out two arrows from his quiver: 'the one to drive love away, the other to cause it'. 'Straightaway was Apollo filled with love, while Daphne, now shunning the very idea of a lover, instead rejoiced in the forest's haunts... Many men sought her hand, but spurning her suitors, she wandered instead through the pathless forests. Unfettered by a husband, she cared not at all for marriage or love or wedded life.' Apollo wooed her with affectionate words, and when that didn't work, he told her about his power, about his father Jupiter, about how medicine was his invention, and how past, present and future are revealed through him. But Daphne was scared, and so she ran away from him. Flight turned her even more beautiful in Apollo's eyes. She ran and Apollo pursued her, she ran until she could run no longer. And then she prayed: 'Open your jaws, oh Earth, and annihilate those looks of mine that cause me such injury.' This is Giesecke's narration of the episode: 'Scarcely did she finish her prayer when a heavy sluggishness overtook her limbs, and her soft chest became enclosed by bark. Her hair grew into leaves, her arms into branches. Her foot, but recently so swift, clung heavily to the earth with roots unyielding, and her face was supplanted by a treetop. Her radiance alone remained intact. Yet even like this Phoebus loved her, and touching the trunk with his right hand, felt her heart still trembling beneath the freshly grown bark. "Though you cannot be my wife," spoke the god to her, "you will be my sacred tree. My hair will always be adorned with your leaves, sweet laurel, as will my cithara and quiver."'

The fear of sexual violence had propelled poor Daphne's desire to turn into a tree. As I read other mythological tales of women turning into trees—of the beautiful and child-like Proserpina, for instance, desired by Saturn's son Pluto who carried her into the underworld, the kingdom of Hades, where she remained in mourning, only to return every six months to her mother, which was when spring arrived on earth, all this because she had tasted the ruby fruit, pomegranate, while in Hades—I began to grow uneasy. That it wasn't women alone who had turned into plants to escape violence did not make me feel any better of course—when Hyacinthus, the handsome Spartan youth with whom Apollo had fallen in love, died, the hyacinth flower sprang from his blood; or when Adonis, for whom Venus even stayed away from the heavens, so much was she enamoured of his beauty, died of injury—'a flower bloomed there, the very colour of blood and like the flowers borne by the pomegranate that conceals its seeds beneath a tough rind', a poppy anemone or the Greek 'windflower' that is terribly vulnerable to the cutting movement of the wind.

While I was revisiting these myths in books and artwork, the morning newspaper brought stories of women who had been raped and murdered, left to die, their bodies chopped and fed to animals, the corpses beheaded and thrown into rivers, 'honour killings' where women were killed by their own family members, fathers, brothers and uncles, then planted into the earth or hanged from trees. My timid escapism and my growing nervousness, this inability to accept the world 'as it is' made me look at these tales in a new, perhaps even strange, way. The girl who had been named 'Nirbhaya' by a permanently excitable Indian media crept into my consciousness repeatedly as I navigated through these stories of transformation, of weakened women who had chosen or been turned into plants to escape sexual violence.

Was it merely a coincidence that Echo was a woman, a creature capable of only repeating line endings, a person without a voice of her own? And was it also only a coincidence that Narcissus, vain Narcissus, was a boy? Echo, who falls in love with the handsome Narcissus and pursues him unabashedly, only to have him hear his own words— 'Someone is here?' 'Someone is here'—in her voice. When nothing comes of that desire, poor Echo covers her face with leaves and retreats into caves until her body wastes away and all that remains is a voice, a sound. Narcissus pays no attention to any of his suitors, not Echo, not his many admirers, both men and women. Rejection of love, for some reason, is looked upon as a terrible insult, and so one of these men gets Nemesis to approve his prayer: 'Let him experience the same sort of love as I: let him not possess the object of his desire!' And so Narcissus falls in love with his own reflection in a pool. The image in the water can, of course, only repeat Narcissus's gestures and actions—images have no souls after all. Narcissus experiences one-sided love in the cruellest way. Like Echo, he withers away, and even after death, when he is carried into the underworld, he cannot help admiring himself in the waters of the Styx. His sisters and their companions weep for him, Echo exaggerates the sound of that weeping with her repetitions. When they come to take his body for the pyre, they find none. 'In its place they found a flower, white petals circling a saffron-yellow centre', the flower narcissus.

What did these tales of transformation mean in an age of cosmetic surgery, makeovers and body surgeries? Why had the people who went through these transformations never exhibited the urge to be a tree or even a flower like narcissus? What had changed so remarkably between Ovid and Lara Croft that the urge to become plant like had been replaced by the urge to look like machines? And yet, there was no culture whose folklore did not have at least one tale where a girl, harassed, killed, or volitionally, had not turned into a tree. There was a version of the Pomegranate Queen tale in every collection I read. In the one collected by the poet and translator A. K. Ramanujan, a stubborn and adamant younger daughter is killed by an angry father because of her refusal to get married. After her body is chopped into pieces and buried in the garden, she emerges as a beautiful pomegranate tree and plays the loveliest music on her veena. Indra, the king of gods, is utterly charmed, and they eventually get married. Not all women-to-tree stories ended with such loaned happiness.

Very few understood that much of my ambition—need—to become a tree was located in the weaknesses of my body. When questioned, I searched for examples. Sometimes I told them about Vansh Pradip Singh, a ruler of the kingdom of Sawar in northern India in the early twentieth century. 'If you cut the smallest branch of a tree it is just as if you cut my finger', he is said to have told his subjects. Ellison Banks Findly, writing about the plant-as-person equivalence in her book, *Plant Lives: Borderline Beings in Indian Traditions*, quotes from the Brihadaranyaka Upanishad: 'As is a mighty tree so indeed is a man.' Thus a person's hairs are the tree's leaves and his skin the outer bark;

and when blood flows from skin, it is as sap flowing from a tree's bark, for 'when a man is wounded blood flows as sap from a tree that is struck'. A person's flesh is the tree's inner bark, his nerves tough like the tree's inner fibres, his bones the wood inside, and his marrow the interior pith. She also quotes this branch of verse from Ramanujan's *Speaking of Siva*:

> The root is the mouth
> of the tree: pour water there
> at the bottom
> and, look, it sprouts green
> at the top.

I sometimes wonder why so many leaves are heart shaped. In poems or moments as short-lived as poems themselves, I have seen the heart move, walk, the entire being turned into this organ that controls life. When I chance upon heart-shaped leaves—and there are too many to name, from the betel leaf to the raspberry—I have the sense of my insides turned out for me to see. I will never know why the walnut resembles the human brain, beans the kidney, bhindis human fingers, and so on. There must be—I want to believe—some relation, even if it is only imaginary. Unlike Jacob Boehme, the German Christian mystic who saw the signature of God in this similarity of shapes and designs, I like to think of this differently—how wonderful it is, I told myself, that I, with my heart and brain and kidneys, am composed of plant parts already.

Sumana Roy

THE SILENCE OF TREES

I need to say it again: among all other desires to become a tree, the most urgent was the need to escape noise. There were two things about this—one was the noise of humans, the other was the vocabulary of silence of the active life of trees. The opposition was terribly stark—the complaining tone that accompanied human work life contrasted with the near silence of the industriousness of trees. I wanted to move to the other side. I was aware of quasi-scientific studies on the effect of music on plant life, how heavy metal, a genre I disliked greatly, had produced the 'best blooms' while plants which had been put on a diet of Cliff Richard, for instance, had perished. Experiments had also turned the biorhythm of plants into a new genre of music. But this did not interest me. For a new habit had begun to take root in my life. I found myself sneaking out my cell phone every time there was a sharp gust of wind.

I wanted to track the reaction of plants to the wind. This interest came to me almost by chance—I had accompanied my family on a trip to the outskirts of our sub-Himalayan Bengal town. Happy to find myself in rural surroundings, one where the intrusion of the human voice could not change the direction of my thoughts, I walked around until I grew tired. It was early spring and the sting of the mid-morning sun was balanced by the sweet wind that blew unobtrusively. I grew infatuated with the soundlessness of the place—no human, animal, bird, automobile or cell phone could wriggle itself into the soundscape here. But it wasn't the taut silence of a prayer hall or examination room. The silence was baggy, and soon a breeze began to gather girth in a bamboo grove under which I stood to give my lungs and feet some rest. I had heard it before, and yet it was unfamiliar—like love, it was old and strange and new at the same time. It was the voice of the bamboo. At first feeble, then strong and commanding, eventually growing careless and losing itself. If I hadn't heard the music of instruments that derive their beauty from the strength of the musician's lungs, I might have thought of this as strange music.

It could be no coincidence that the most beautiful musical instruments had been created out of plant life. The flute, storing the wind in it, and then breathing it out in installments—the equivalence of the bamboo being a giant flute did not come to me then. For it wasn't the giant bamboos that spoke but their leaves. They fluttered in the wind, they complained about it, they grew used to it, they grew indifferent to it. In my mind, the complaint of the leaves, like the shehnai at Hindu weddings, became a song about an absent lover who did not know the discipline of love, and so arrived and left without routine or schedule.

Perhaps I imagined too much. But that started a habit. I recorded the sound of the crisp bamboo leaves moving in the wind—there was something delightfully sensuous and sexual in their refusal to be tamed, and also something terribly sad in the way they let the wind leave them and move on to a neighbouring lover. I recorded the sound of that meeting—mating?—between the leaves and the wind. Later, in the relative quiet of the evening at home, when the dark gradually swallowed the noises of daylight, I watched the video. Then I closed my eyes and listened to the sounds. Though no one would have guessed it, except master sound artists in studios perhaps, I could make out my gasping at two places in this short one-minute video. I felt sad and even envious: why could I not react to the wind like the leaves of the bamboo?

Since then I have been on many sound-catching mini expeditions. Just as music teachers categorize human voices as belonging to different 'scales', I began calibrating the reactions of different tree leaves to the wind. Dry sal leaves have the highest pitched voice and long stemmed grasses, drying at the tip, are terribly shrill. Unlike the music teacher, I haven't named these characteristic sounds after letters of the alphabet.

Sumana Roy

In fact, I've done quite the opposite. I have begun categorizing the voices of people on their tonal proximity to the sound of leaves in the wind. My father's baritone, for instance, is of the sal leaves, my mother's is of the jamun leaves, my little nephew's affectionate mewling the voice of ankle-length grass. My husband, after he'd chuckled at my weird nomenclature, said that he'd found the plant life equivalent of my voice too: I have the voice of 'dhaaner khetey dheu', the wind waves on paddy fields.

Sometimes I gave up. Not out of frustration but because recording would take away from the joy of experiencing. One day in March, I was alone in a forest, not completely inside it, but not on the margins either. A kalbaishakhi, a northwester, came without warning. I had spent much of my morning recording the crunchy sound of dried leaves. Just as human hair grows thinner as it grows towards gravity, a tree thins out as it moves away from gravity. And so the trembling and shaking is highest at the tip of a tree. I had no apparatus with which to record the sound of that tremulousness, that diffidence against gravity. I tried to climb on to a neighbouring tree without much success. A few feet above the ground, in spite of sitting in the tree's valley, I felt scared of being dislodged by the ferociousness of the wind. For a moment I found myself wondering whether trees suffer from vertigo. Or whether a windless day put them in a trance. This sense of keeping my ears tuned to the rustle of the leaves brought a new dimension to my living.

I had, in frustration with industrial noise and human verbosity, mistaken trees as silent creatures. My experiments with the sound recorder had brought about a new realization—that trees shared a natural sound with people. It is the sound of resistance—like protesters 'raising their voice', trees produced a sound that held in it their fight against wind, water, rain, to tearing, cutting and breaking. Like everything else, about sound too, they were economical. Revolution. Rebellion. Resistance. All other sounds were noise.

🌱

The question began to come gradually, and then often. Which tree did I want to be? I still have no answer. How was I to explain that it did not matter to me whether I was a tall tree, a middling shrub or grass or garden weed? The lack of merit lists in the plant universe had drawn me towards it. The French philosophers Gilles Deleuze and Félix Guattari have written poetically and passionately about the rhizome—say, ginger or turmeric—as a model to oppose the hierarchies and power structures of the tree model that holds Western civilization together. The rhizome, without beginning or end, without the privileging of top over bottom or one 'branch' over another, is a moral about subverting hierarchies. For me it did not matter—this was as much man-made appropriation as the tree had been for centuries. When asked to choose between tall trees and short grass, for instance, naturalist Hal Borland's telling words often came to my rescue: 'Knowing trees, I understand the meaning of patience. Knowing grass, I can appreciate persistence.'

When I eventually decided to write about my experience of metamorphosis, my spiritual and emotional transformation into a tree, I wasn't sure whether I could use the word 'literature' at all. It seemed so artificial, not just the scaffolding of voice and structure, but this whole thing about genre. 'The very concept of genre is as cold as the tomb,' said Andrei Tarkovsky. In my mind it was a version of racism in literature and the arts, this tendency to segregate on the basis of length, intention, voice, and perhaps ambition. I was certain, of course, only in the way such certitude is possible, that there was no natural division of genres—grass as poem and banyan as epic, ginger as philosophical tract and rose as young adult fiction? Or the nine o'clock flowers as day genre and the night queen flowers as examples of the night genre? When I read any book these days, a section titled 'Acknowledgements' inevitably prefixes or suffixes the primary text. Who would feature in such a list if a tree were to write a note of gratitude? The sun, the rain, the gardener, the bees, the birds, humans, the wind, and so on? And wouldn't every tree have the same list of 'acknowledgements' then? Such comic thoughts were immediately reined in by stony realism: acknowledgements as a genre in its own right did not—could not— exist in the plant world. Another component of the writing process

Part II

I Paint Flowers So They Will Not Die
—Frida Kahlo

DRAWING TREES

For many years, unaware of where the impulse came from, I had taken photographs of trees with the energy of portrait makers. When I looked at the photos on my computer screen, they, abetted by the quick energy of the right arrow key, looked like something that was part of a design, one I had not seen move inside my consciousness. Without realizing it, I had been photographing dead trees for nearly a decade, perhaps longer. I wanted to find out why. What was it about bare trees, shorn and leafless, that had attracted my eye? Pathetic fallacy being one of my great vices, I tried to spot whether this visual attraction for the lifeless had anything to do with my iterant melancholic urges.

The human equivalent of the bare trees, many of them dead but still standing with borrowed dignity, would be skeletons. A diet of ghost stories, most of them from the house help, for the most part immigrants from Bangladesh who seemed quite bent on revealing the scariness of their former country, had shaped my natural timidity into a morbid fear of ghosts. I would never understand why humans without flesh and skin—that was, after all, the only difference between ghosts and living bodies—should scare me. It was difficult for me to imagine myself photographing a ghost or human corpses, but I had spent hours (which over time added up to months and then years) moving around dead trees, looking for the perfect angle that would capture the beauty of their branches, actually the beauty of the geometry of a dead body. This beauty of bareness I began to see later as the beauty of barrenness, say, the beauty of a desert, for in being shorn of flowers and leaves, these trees had managed to escape the burden and technology of reproduction. These postmenopausal trees gradually grew into statues in my eyes. And with that thought came the question—why are there no statues of trees?

In street corners, inside museums and temples, even in drawing rooms, there are sculptures of humans, men, women, sometimes with children, of their things, vases and musical instruments. But where were the statues of trees? How—and why—had the visual culture of humans neglected the transformation of nature into culture when it came to trees?

I distinctly remember my first lessons at drawing a tree. My mother was my first art teacher, this only by virtue of the fact that adults think they can draw better than children. In her world, which was no different from that of most adults, there were only three kinds of trees—a tree, a generic tree with a stout brown trunk, curved to resemble a woman's waist, and on top of it a heavy mop of curly green hair; the second was a simple depiction of the palm, what passed for coconut trees in children's drawing books, a long line holding smaller thread-like arced lines, and often hanging from below the conglomeration of assembled leaf-lines, roundish coconuts defying gravity and the glue of lines that join things in paintings; the third was the child's version of the conifer, a short stump and staircases from either side meeting to a climax at the top, where the angel stands on a Christmas tree. All three kinds grew close to where I lived, this being the fertile foothills of the Himalayas that allowed for a certain variety of cosmopolitanism in the plant world. But my mother was not bothered about this—she did not ask us to draw trees while looking at them. It seemed to have been decided, in some pedagogical universe, that these were children's drawing book trees. Of course, I did not think of it then, but it makes me curious now, especially when I see my three-year-old nephew draw unrelated lines and pass them off as leaves. I wonder how a child 'sees' a tree.

For, when I was in Class Three, our drawing teacher in school threatened to punish me if I did not draw a proper tree. There are some phrases that form hives in our consciousness—her 'dancing leaves' is one such. The leaves on my art book tree refused to stand still—it

Sumana Roy

might have been my belief in the inherent mobility of leaves, but given how young I was, it must have been just an unsteady hand trying to tame a runaway pencil.

'Whenever I want to draw a tree,' I remember saying, 'the leaves move'.

'Draw a leafless tree,' my closest friend whispered in my ear. 'Then she won't scold you.'

And then she drew a few quasi-triangles near the foot of the tree—they were fallen leaves.

I never got good grades in art competitions in school. I only drew leaves, a fat midriff with taut veins, their individual ambitions held in check by a margin which suddenly changed lines of that colony into a leaf. The drawings were all wrong, I was told from time to time—both of the margin, and the veins within. That was how it ought to be, I wanted to say but I refrained from doing so. I still do not know why. Was it claustrophobia that stopped me from limiting the growth of the leaves? Whatever it might have been, it did not stop me from pursuing an amateur's career of drawing leaves, and leaves alone.

But more than the drawing was the impulse for collecting leaves, leaves of different ages and parents. These leaves are still with me. Time has eaten away their flesh, leaving only the scaffolding on which life was held together. When I look at some of the old greetings cards these leaves now survive on, I see them as proud soldiers that have become memorialized into statues. Because I could not draw them as well as my peers did, I turned to the 'original' and wanted to make them art. I was embarrassed, though, by the realization that I loved my leaves so much I had to kill them.

For the parallel history of my childhood, dotted as it is with distant commendations about my quietness and kindness, must also take into account these aged dictionaries and encyclopaedias, my weapons of murder. What could be a child's joy in eroding a leaf of its greenness? Was I only mimicking my paternal grandmother who crushed a red hibiscus between the pages of her husband's used ledgers every single day of her married life, this by her own account? I no longer remember even the hint of joy that might have attended the flaunting of the skeletons of leaves from inside my books, the kind that makes a child a momentary hero to her friends. The truth is that I don't remember any of my friends caring much about these dead leaves. If my exhibits had been animals, cockroaches or ants even, their young jaws might have dropped or their mouths opened in awe. But who cared for skeletons of leaves? They were worthless—no one would be scared of them.

The awareness of romantic love would increase the worth of these history-pressed leaves to me. Melancholia being significant fodder to romantic love, these leaves suddenly became beautiful to me. Prone to emotional excess, I began to question why lovers should gift flowers to each other—flowers were, after all, short-lived, all things nouveau, even younger than their relationship. Skeletal leaves, brittle with age, remnants of a lover's childhood that one had not been part of—those would certainly make better gifts? But I found no lover who thought of leaves, particularly dead leaves, as romantic presents.

I continued to draw leaves on my clothes and my mother's saris, and would have done the same on my brother's and father's shirts and kurtas had their notions of masculinity not made them think of leaves (oddly, because to all intents and purposes they are without sex) as feminine.

What I did not realize for some years was my complete indifference to what is perhaps a tree's most important part—the roots. Not a single teacher had spent any kind of energy in teaching me how to draw plant roots. In the hierarchy of plant parts, the root was literally at the lowest. When has art cared for the hidden or the invisible? If you couldn't see it, you didn't need to draw it. It wasn't only that perhaps—any assemblage of lines could pass for roots. The arbitrary and unpredictable character of roots was both their virtue and vice in art. Imagine drawing human footsteps, like people draw the goddess Lakshmi's footprints on a full moon night—the parallel career of footsteps, pretty to the eye but also boring because of its predictability, how the pair of feet must travel together always. The branches of roots do not travel together but in different directions—they are solitary explorers.

So when nine-year-old Puja, our cook's granddaughter, told me that the 'first boy' in her class had been punished for drawing roots for a tree, I was surprised. Why had he been punished? 'Because he had signed his name below the painting of the tree root.' I wondered what could be wrong with that, this early, even hilarious, manifestation of authorship.

'No, you don't get it,' explained the nine-year-old girl to me. 'His name is Shikawr (roots). The teacher thought he was being smart—writing his name to explain what he was drawing.'

'And how was his drawing?' I wanted to know.

'How do you think it was? An ugly brownish black thing. How can roots be beautiful?'

Two things struck me immediately: how tree roots never get a pedicure; and how the names of flowers are chosen for girls and the 'ugly brownish black' root for boys. The poor 'first boy' had perhaps only wanted the root—his name Shikawr—to become visible.

'The teacher called him names.'

'Names?'

'Yes,' she said—'Eesh, our Nandalal Bose.'

Puja's education had not acquainted her with the name of Nandalal Bose. She thought it a harsh scolding, like calling someone 'Buddhuram Pandey', an imagined name for a foolish man, for instance.

Who was Nandalal Bose and why had Puja's art teacher brought up his name?

My mother grew up in Santiniketan, and the names of painters and sculptors from Visva-Bharati, the university founded by Rabindranath Tagore, were almost colloquial in our house. But my brother and I had no shorthand education in art history. Ramkinkar and Nandalal were names and names alone. My parents must have been too involved in preparing us for professional careers to notice these lapses.

My father's closest friend was a zoologist, and whenever he visited us from Calcutta, he carried gifts for us—the most precious of these were his travel stories. What my brother and I loved best was his use of drawings to illustrate his storytelling. He would sketch landscapes and people while telling us about them—motion pictures of the best kind. One day Kamalesh-jethu drew a picture of two trees. One looked terribly tiny compared to the other. The large tree had tiny leaves—he said it was a tree from the Sahara Desert. The smaller one, that looked like a dwarf in comparison to the 'African' tree, was a 'miniature', he explained. It was a Chinese tree. In the 1980s, Made-in-China was exotic, Chinese fountain pens, Chinese silk, and so on. We were enamoured of the Chinese tree—my brother was quick with interpretations. The tiny leaves on the tree were the equivalent of Mongoloid eyes, he reasoned.

What stayed with me from that storytelling was not so much the story—the battle between the African and Chinese trees (I cannot remember who won)—as the lesson he gave us about drawing a tree. It came to him from the film-maker Satyajit Ray, he told us. Nandalal Bose had been Ray's teacher at Visva-Bharati and had told him this: 'Not from the top downwards. A tree grows up, not down. The strokes must be from the base upwards...' I'd discover this line later, in Ray's *Our Films, Their Films*, and the memory of Kamalesh-jethu's right hand pulling lines from top to bottom to mimic the movement of growth from seedling to sapling and eventually to a grown-up tree would return.

When I would, many years later, read *Trees of Santiniketan* during a long stay in Santiniketan, I'd begin to look at the old trees in a strange way. In my gaze would always be the question—how might Nandalal Bose have looked at them?

A few things about Nandalal Bose's life must be mentioned here. Born in Bihar in the late nineteenth century, Bose was a student of Abanindranath Tagore, master teacher and nephew of Rabindranath Tagore, who prevailed upon him to teach at his university in Santiniketan. Nandalal's best loved work, his portrayals of village life, are now considered amongst the most remarkable modernist paintings in India.

Almost completely by chance, I landed upon Nandalal's essays on drawing trees. The artist and critic K. G. Subramanyan had translated Bose's essays into English for a volume published by the Visva-Bharati Publishing Department. I had looked for it in many libraries, but it wasn't to be found. So when the proprietor of Subarnarekha, a bookstore close to Rabindra Bhavan, handed me a copy on a dark power-cut evening in March, it was as if I had at last discovered a long lost relative.

Needless to say, I spent that night without sleep. Nandalal's magical and even mysterious formulae for making paint from plant 'products' would come later. But before that I had to find out what he thought of trees. In these curiosities, I found myself behaving like a lover. I was eager for some kind of kinship—lovers are, after all, relatives in a shared universe. And there is such happiness—even relief—in loving a loved one for the same reasons.

'A tree grows upward; it is driven by a singular urge to spread towards the sky—trunk, branch and leaf.' This is the opening line of the chapter 'The Structure and Characteristics of Plants and Trees'. In it is empathy and identification, yes—it holds the ambition of the tree, to defy gravity and 'grow upward'. The painter Nandalal has already become a tree by the time he came to writing this. For both the tree and the painter are clients of light. Chlorophyll and canvas—both are functions and consequences of light. Light—the tree's food, the painter's kitchen. And so Nandalal's concern is only with the visible tree. Roots do not interest him because they are not creatures of light.

What follows next is more evidence of the greed for light: 'All its branches and all the leaves and flowers on its twigs and stems grow in such a way as to get as much sunlight as possible; this is why its branches, its twigs, flowers and fruits emerge in a spiral motion from the (parent) trunk, branch or twig, respectively. To absorb, as much as possible, the rays of the sun, its life-giver, with all its body, then grow big and bear fruit is its natural urge.' There can be no doubt that Nandalal is speaking as a tree. I recognized my ancestry in love immediately: how could I forget the number of times I had moved the window curtains away to let sunlight fall on a light-hungry houseplant the way I might have done the opposite—drawing the curtains together—to guard my infant nephew's sleep from the light?

I am still unsure whether Nandalal has become the tree or he has made the tree become Nandalal when the second paragraph arrives:

'The trunk is like the tree's backbone; so its characteristic rhythm has to be drawn first'. Tree as mammal, tree as man. I paused on older reflections, of similar anthropocentric thoughts, of wondering, even worrying, about the tree's 'back' itching and no one to scratch it. With an annoyance that time hasn't cooled completely, my mother remembers an incident from my childhood when she found the leaves of a hibiscus shrub smeared yellow with Burnol, a cream used to treat superficial burns. Maya-mashi, our aged house help, had poured warm water on the plant in the garden and no one had bothered to offer any first aid, I explained to my mother. What else could I have done? My mother's list of my 'gechho'—plant—eccentricities is long. But it is impossible for me to see them as aberrations. When my mother-in-law first visited my parents to discuss the marriage between her son and me, my mother, instead of highlighting my virtues, as might be expected, warned her about my attachment to plants. To an outsider it might have seemed like she was speaking of an affair that her daughter was involved in, Radha's mother complaining about her daughter's restless pining for Krishna.

Nandalal's advice about drawing different varieties of trees begins to sound, at least to my mind, like a master telling his students how to draw different types of gymnasts and acrobats in an Olympic stadium: 'So some tree trunks grow twisting up; some seem swollen with veins; some (like the shimul) stand straight and steady like the central pole of a tent, clutching the earth and keeping its balance in the same manner.' Trees are persons with different kinds of personalities, and every time I read these portions from Nandalal, I sat upright, held my spine rigid like a flag pole and thought of our P. T. teacher in school who said that he could write character certificates of each of us from the way we walked and held our spine. 'Bamboo, Nim, Palmyra and similar trees follow another system. That an iron pipe is stronger than an iron rod is a well-known fact. So the hollow trunks of the palm or the bamboo are stronger than sal stems of comparable girth.' Can I be blamed for thinking of the tallest gymnasts in school when I read this line from Nandalal? Or that I think of an aged grandparent in a hospital bed being fed through tubes through his or her nose when

I read Nandalal's description of the banyan tree's 'numerous mouths' or of an aged relative on crutches when the words about 'save itself from collapse' come in the following line? 'A banyan tree spreads its branches wide on all sides, but to save itself from collapse from the weight of matter and age, it drops roots at regular intervals; in time these grow big and prop (up) the heavy, old branches like pillars, and suck food from the earth with numerous mouths.'

In the tutorial sketches of the trees that accompany Nandalal's words, the trees are no longer just trees. They are human or animal like. The lines used to draw 'trunks: teak, silk, cotton, banyan', for instance, are very similar to the lines used to draw the figure of a woodcutter in the background in the same frame—the limbs of the man and the tree trunk resemble each other in the way human siblings often do. In an illustration on how to draw small twigs, Nandalal draws a small twig and a snake beside each other, and it is difficult to tell one from the other. The words accompanying the illustration make the same plant-animal equivalence: 'Small twigs emerge from a branch like spines from a snake's backbone. Like a snake, a branch, too, has a back and belly side, the top open to light, the bottom bound in shadow.'

The Sanskrit word for this kind of kinship is 'sahrydaya', the co-soul, the soulmate, the sharer of the soul. Discovering a sahrydaya in Nandalal brought such relief and joy: I was not the only one who had regarded the tree as a human or the human as a tree. I turn a page, and there is Nandalal again, showing students how to draw tree joints. I smile at the kinship, the reference to 'human' in the instruction: 'All those special arrangements to strengthen a branch at the joint! Human carpenters seem to have learnt their lessons from trees.' The tree-becoming human is also on the next page where the illustration of tree bark made me want to scratch a rough patch of skin on my knee, where so many scars of childhood games live: 'The edges of scars resulting from the stripping of barks from tree trunks seem to have been sewn up and repaired.' And before this bit of excitement has settled in and I've begun investigating my knees for the bark they might be, the next page pulls me by the ear, almost literally. In this tutorial on how to draw 'knots of trees' is the close-up of a knot that is difficult to tell from a human ear.

Nandalal gives us both in his instructor notes—the 'right' and the 'wrong'. Tree-branch joints, for instance, are not a simplistic function of straight lines, a 'Y' or half an 'H'. This distinction between 'right' and 'wrong' lines immediately reminded me of the difference between the strong lines on a fashion designer's drafts and their eventual translation to the sweet curves on a garment when they sit on a human model. Another fascinating distinction that the painter brings to our attention is one between the dead and the living. In this too, I notice how he sees no distinction between plants and humans: life has curves, a bend in a stem, a crouching flower; death is a straight line, it makes the living fall flat and limp.

In the illustrative section titled 'Tree Forms in Traditional Art', Nandalal shows how generic trees have been drawn in various cultures—the palm-like fronds of Harappa, the branched bolus of 1000 BCE Egypt, the clump of leaves of the 200 BCE Sanchi Stupa, the colony of trees headed by a tall leader of Florence, the 'conceptual, not merely decorative' twirls of Jain art, the decorative efflorescence of a multitude of leaves in Rajasthani art, the austere sketch of a tree in Persian art and how that gathers foliage in Kangra art, the 'distant tree' of Mughal art, the terribly decorative leaves and trees of late Persian art and so on. This is neither pure botany nor art history—this is a plant-life equivalent of the Museum of Man.

It is not only this plant-as-person equivalence that made me kin to Nandalal. It was the way he had looked at the world—how could it be, I wondered, as I grazed through his writings and tutorials, that he had spotted a tree, a leaf, a flower, a plant, in everything, like I did? In a section titled 'Improvised Conventions', Nandalal directs us to take 'lessons from Nature', in how 'its rhythms have developed amongst different people in different times and places under the influence of natural environment or human history'. And then he decides to illustrate his words—when I first looked at these drawings, I forgot to breathe. Nandalal had drawn a medium-sized 'kalka', a paisley, and a woman inside it. Yes, a woman. Adjacent to it was a line drawing of the

Buddha, and around him was a margin that had turned Gautama into a flower—'the bell of the lotus'. The third drawing on the page was that of a minor god or perhaps even a king, the kind we encounter in the Ellora caves, for instance. The margin around this god, meant to imitate the shape of the sculpture, is exactly like a broad leaf—Nandalal will not let us miss that at all. 'Manasa or katmallika leaf' run the words below the drawing. On the next page is a drawing of a woman that looks like a collage of flowers and petals: the folds of the woman's sari near the thighs as she squats on the floor resemble two leaves with prominent veins; the loose end of her head veil ends in a paisley pattern. Her hands resemble leaves, her feet petals. Below it is Nandalal's telling instruction: 'This drawing (of the woman) has many angular breaks like petals or flowers.' K. G. Subramanyan, in a biographical sketch of Nandalal, mentions 'how he was once impressed by gnarled roots of a tree but brought its quality into the drawing of the wrinkled face of a woman'. Woman as plant: the man had known me before I'd discovered myself.

Nandalal, like me, had seen the form of trees in everything, like Meerabai had seen her Rana, her god, in the world around her. He saw trees in mountains. It's a brilliant manual on how to draw mountains: if you've mastered the art of drawing plant life, you'd know how to draw mountains too, he explains. The accompanying illustrations are self-explanatory, with inverted trees resembling mountains and mountain peaks resembling lotus buds, but so are the notes:

- To paint the shaded valleys on mountain sides, one can paint trees upside down.
- Trees and bushes cluster in those portions of the valley where the streams flow...
- Light falling on the sides of a mountain takes the shape of an upright tree touched with light; not downwards as in the case of valleys.
- Indian mountains look like lotus buds. This is the reason why our temple spires too are so designed to resemble mountain peaks.

Nandalal spends several pages on the last, on how to draw lotus buds, its petals, the flower in bloom, noting its primacy in Hindu and Buddhist art. The truth is that in spite of my deep empathetic reading of Nandalal's work, I did not learn to draw plants any better. But this close communion with someone with whom I was certain I shared an ancestry of chlorophyll made me look at the world anew: I, who had found a tree in every face on the wall and every cloud in the sky, had never managed to notice what Nandalal Bose did: 'The cone is the symbol of fire...When it is burning steadily like a flame it is shaped like an upturned bud or banana flower.'

K. G. Subramanyan, in his biographical sketch of Nandalal, further mentions: 'He had, as he mentioned to a close friend, started to see his Siva in trees...' I wasn't surprised. It is all there, in his drawings and paintings of plant life, the 'Dolan Champa Flower', 'Fruit Gathering', and perhaps the most famous of them all, the employment of plants in the large mural in Sriniketan to commemorate the first 'Halakarsna Utsav', the ploughing ceremony in the agriculture school. When Subramanyan quotes Nandalal on tradition, the same metaphors strike root:'For tradition is the outer shell of the seed that holds the embryo of new growth...'; or when writing about his guru Abanindranath's work, these words to his friend Kanai Samanta—'it is silent like the light of dawn, like the unfolding of a flower or the sprouting of a seed'. It is almost a transferred epithet then, when Rabindranath Tagore employs the same tropes to praise Nandalal's contribution to Visva-Bharati: 'In this atmosphere one of my barren branches has suddenly borne fruit, like the bamboo which after a long period suddenly blossoms into flowers before ending its game of life.'

That Nandalal thought of trees as persons is evident from this anecdote that Subramanyan narrates to us:

> Talking to a student who is studying a tree he says, 'Watch the tree for some time. Go and sit near it, morning, noon and evening, even in the darkness of the night. That will not be easy. After sitting for a while you will feel bored. You will feel that the tree is telling you in annoyance, "What are you doing here? Go away! Get lost!" Then you will have to coax the tree. And say,

Sumana Roy

"My teacher has asked me to. I cannot but heed him. Please bear with me. Be nice to me, show yourself to me." If after a few days of such effort you feel you are seeing the tree, then go home, close yourself up and paint that tree.'

I knew that I would paint a tree someday.

MAKING LEAVES

The greatest perpetrator of lookism in our times is, of course, the photograph, especially as it plays out on social media. Apart from Beauty, what is being shown is Happiness. And so the ubiquitous 'group photograph' with family and friends. But my family does not consist of human members alone—there are my potted plants and trees. Would a photograph with them be considered a 'family photograph'? And now that it had become mandatory to smile in such photographs—why do we have to smile in our photographs when we rarely do so in life outside a photograph is something that I shall never quite understand—what would my plants do, having never learnt to say 'cheese'? I did post a photo of myself with a few of my plants, but, quite naturally, the comments were either about me or about the 'freshness' and 'colour' of the flowers and so on. Not a single person said anything about this being a happy family photograph.

There is another genre that speaks of our obsessions: the photograph with the 'celebrity'. More often than not, it is a selfie with a famous person, man, woman, child, wax statue. Are there celebrity trees? I stood in and under one once, in Bodh Gaya, the Mahabodhi Tree. I've never been envious of people standing beside their favourite celebrities in photographs—distance is often a good thing, especially in such non-relationships. Posing with strangers is embarrassing, as I found out on that afternoon in Bodh Gaya. There were many like me, who would need to annotate the photograph with arrow marks in their conversation forever. There wouldn't be anyone who'd say, as they might had I been standing next to a human celebrity: 'Ah, how lucky you are to be standing next to Amitabh Bachchan'. That is the truth—

there are no celebrity trees. And that was a good thing—for more than anything else, I had sought the anonymity of trees. Even paintings and photographs had not been able to steal that away from them.

My mother wears a pair of gold leaves on her ears. They are old, having come as a gift from my father on their first wedding anniversary. The earrings are set in stone—two tiny diamonds and another tiny ruby as the third leaf. Though it is difficult to imagine it now, my father was a romantic lover once. My mother remembers the words that accompanied the gift not with fondness but curiosity, as if they carried a mystery that she no longer has any use for: 'Leaves for your ears, so that they bring in birdsong...' She was stupefied, she is now pleased to report, like a grand old dame who always knew that romance was a sham—she did not care for jewellery, she did not care for birdsong either. But what had annoyed her most was the certainty of her husband's foolishness. The goldsmith had passed off earrings that were actually representations of the three eyes of the Goddess Durga as three leaves.

Two eyes with a third in between, like two leaves and a bud-like leaf. The couple argued about their different interpretations; no consensus has yet been reached in their forty-two-year-old marriage. One of the arguments that my mother offered has been a mainstay in their marriage: 'A woman is like a tree. Her heart, her mind, her hands, her feet, all these are also like parts of trees or trees themselves.'

My father, who in his mind has never lost a debate, inevitably sneaks in an annoying bit: 'And eyes? And ears?'

My mother will only catch the first of these nouns and retort, 'Women have three eyes, like two leaves and that bud in between.'

And suddenly she would remove her earrings from her earlobes to demonstrate her anger.

My father is not one to give up. 'If only the tree could get rid of its leaves so easily.'

My brother and I know the staple of this inconsequential word parade. There will be silence for some time, and then the scraping of steel utensils in the kitchen, until my father would say, 'My grandfather came from a family of goldsmiths. And people think that I don't know what makes a gold leaf.'

Too young to understand the grease of pet grudges and their iterant complaints that keep a marriage in the living room and not the attic as it were, I could never get why such a fuss had to be made over leaves, that too those that had not performed the most important function of their leaf life: photosynthesis.

My father once took me to a goldsmith's tiny workshop, and there I watched the man, on my father's instructions and measurements, blow fire into a plate of silver, pull at it, scold the metal and pet it, from several sides and angles, until it cooled and turned into silver leaves. Dust and dirt have now settled into the silver veins of my silver leaf earrings. Two things bother me about the life of these leaves that hung from my ears once: how fire was responsible for their birth, as sunlight is to the birth of chlorophyll leaves; and how leaves, when turned into art, whether as jewellery or as motif in sculptures, in spite of their quiet dignity, are always marginalized. On panels in art and sculpture, a row of patterned leaves will act as a frame and, most often, only that. Or leaves are inevitably transformed into ornamental paisleys, neither leaf nor flower, a hybrid without soul, for this I have known always—paisleys can have no soul.

Meaning and its consequences must be reserved for flowers or tree trunks. Leaves are factories, industrial houses without the surplus of fantastic symbolism, the constancy of their green uniform is no propellant for the imagination. In folk art, especially as they play out on alpana and rangoli on the floor, a few strokes indicate a stem of leaves—it's like a corridor, it must lead to something more meaningful, like fruits or flowers. I am always piqued and saddened when I see the drawing books of beginners in art school—my nephew, for instance, was taught how to draw and 'colour' an apple first, then a generic flower. There are no pages indicating lessons on how to draw leaves.

A eunuch at a road-crossing in Calcutta once told me this, when I told her that I loved the leaves on her green sari: 'Flowers are women, they seduce. Leaves are male, they work hard to impress. I have to be both.'

I remember looking at her curly hair and wondering why children are always taught to draw the human face first, and so little energy is spent on drawing human hair. Then, almost as if on cue, she took off her wig of long hair and wiped the sweat off her shaven head with the loose end of her sari.

The hair and the feet. Leaves and roots. They are not worth the primary-school art teacher's attention.

For a school concert where O. Henry's *The Last Leaf* was to be dramatized, my classmates and I were instructed to make leaves. We had all drawn leaves, of course, and so we thought it would be easy— cutting those leaves drawn on paper. There was nothing special about a conglomerate of leaves—to our child minds, they might as well have been mass-produced factory items, like nuts and bolts. And so we began cutting out leaves from art paper. But these paper leaves had no veins as scaffolding and so curled at the edges. Real leaves did not behave like that, of course, except if they were going through the process of drying.

Only one leaf was to be special.

The last leaf.

The leaves in O. Henry's short story are fall leaves, in different stages of drying, but our paper leaves could not replicate that. That made us aware of the importance of veins like no biology lesson could have. I looked at my hand—in my mind these were the closest relatives of leaves. Without bones, paper hands would also be without character and structure. The art and craft teacher was summoned. Paper leaves were useless, she said. Cloth, satin in particular, would be the closest in texture to the glossy texture of leaves. But below each leaf, like a stretcher carrying it, was to be an amateur mesh of thin tin wires, performing the role of veins. Disobedience to the dictum came in several forms: a few used match sticks instead of wires, their parents having forbidden them to use sharp-ended wires. The best came from

Saroj—she had glued dry twigs onto the backs of the cloth leaves. And so the responsibility of making the 'last leaf' fell to Saroj. I did not see it then, of course, but I can now—the fascinating play of art imitating life and art imitating that art. The plot of O. Henry's story is simple: Sue and Johnsy are artists who live in New York City's Greenwich Village. Sue wants to paint pictures for stories in magazines while Johnsy wants to visit Italy and paint the Bay of Naples. It is a terribly harsh winter in the 1890s and Johnsy gets pneumonia. The doctor says medicines won't help her unless she wants to get better. A little later, Sue finds Johnsy speaking to herself. The girl is counting backwards: twelve, and then eleven, and ten and so on.

> 'There are only five leaves left now,' said Johnsy.
> 'Five what, dear? Tell your Sudie.
> 'Leaves. On the ivy vine. When the last one falls I must go, too.
> I have known that for three days. The last leaf will fall soon and
> then I'll die. Didn't the doctor tell you?'

Johnsy has begun to believe in her life—and death—being a mimicry of the life of leaves on the tree in winter. In that she has become the tree. Sue tries to convince her and fails. Later that evening, she visits Behrman, their aged downstairs neighbour, an artist 'who was a failure in art' but was 'always about to' paint a masterpiece. Sue tells him about the moral poor Johnsy has attached to the falling of leaves. How is she to be saved?

> 'Oh, the foolish girl!' Behrman shouted. 'An old vine can't kill
> people!'
> 'She's very ill and weak', said Sue, 'and the fever has left her
> mind morbid and full of strange fancies.'

That night there was storm and rain and Johnsy woke up waiting to die, for the last leaf to fall. For all the leaves had fallen off that tree, all but one. The next night there was more rain and yet the stubborn leaf didn't fall. Johnsy begins to realize that she had been wrong: 'I've been a very foolish girl, Sue,' she said. 'I wanted to die. But the last leaf has stayed on the vine. It has taught me a lesson. Please, bring me a bowl of soup now.'

Along with this comes another piece of information: Behrman is dead. A ladder was found in his yard. And a lamp and paintbrushes and green and yellow paint. Sue stitches the pieces of information together: 'Look at the last leaf on the vine. It's still there. It has never moved in the wind. Didn't that surprise you? It's Behrman's masterpiece, dear. He painted it on the night of the storm.'

There were only five characters in the play—I had wanted to play Sue; so many of my friends used that nickname for me—I was greedy. But the role went to one of the prettiest girls in class, a girl so beautiful that we sometimes stared at her in wonder. The inexplicability of beauty and its lack of democracy came to us at such cruel moments, when roles in plays were handed out by teachers. The rest of the class had only one role to play—we were to become mini Behrmans, producing leaves in bulk. Saroj brought Behrman's last leaf to class a few days before the concert. We were forbidden to touch it. Sanchita, the only girl in our class who had been abroad, complained aloud to the teacher: 'It's only a fake leaf, ma'am,' she said. 'Why treat it like a museum artefact?' I remember being stunned, not by the difficult words in her argument but her courage. In my mind, I passed on the role of Sue to her.

I laugh as I write this now, recollecting the events leading to the final show. How two able-bodied pedestal fans from the wings on the stage rehearsed playing the role of the windy storm of a December night in nineteenth-century New York. How our lightly glued leaves fell in that storm. How Saroj's Hercules Leaf remained stuck in spite of all the drama by air. I noticed Saroj's face beaming with pride at the end of every rehearsal—she had become the leaf. On the last school day of December, before the start of the winter vacation, the play was finally staged. Our classmates did not have to act out their shivering— the cold gusts of pedestal fan breeze left their sweater-covered bodies cold. They looked natural. Even the leaves—our leaves—fell with swift timidity, like actors to whom the role came 'naturally'. Behrman's leaf—Saroj's leaf—weathered the fan-storm. Until it too fell, just before Sue's last dialogue about the painter's 'masterpiece'. Those in the audience who were not aware of O. Henry's story, thus went back home with a different ending from those who knew the story and realized that there had been a goof up. The last leaf had given a terrible performance. It would have to be replaced by a new actor for the next show.

THE LITERATURE OF TREES

Trees are faceless. It was perhaps this that had brought me to them, to escape the scrutiny of the face. Photographs, drawings and paintings of plant life had brought home lessons: flowers are perhaps more photographed than faces. But trees? Any 'scenery' must have a tree—such goes the adult dictum. For the first few years of our lives, our parents and teachers compel us to draw more trees than we draw human faces our entire lives.

Manuel Lima, named as one of the 'fifty most creative and influential minds of 2009' in a survey by *Creativity* magazine, explores more than 800 years of the tree diagram in his terrific book, *The Book of Trees: Visualizing Branches of Knowledge*. Lima writes that the tree is 'one of the most popular, captivating, and widespread visual archetypes', and includes in his fun and exhaustive survey its different types—figurative trees, vertical trees, horizontal trees, multidirectional trees, radial trees, hyperbolic trees, rectangular tree maps, Voronoi Treemaps, circular tree maps, sunbursts, and icicle trees. Ben Shneiderman, in the foreword to Lima's book, tells us about his innovative work with computers and how he was led to use the tree as a structure:

> The recursive branching structure of trees, which provides a compelling metaphor for organizing knowledge, was at the forefront of my mind as I developed the rectangular tree map as a means to display the nested structure of folders on a computer's hard drive. My innovation went beyond turning a three-dimensional tree into a nested planar diagram; I was eager to show the leafiness of each branch as an area whose relative size showed the magnitude of that leafiness. Furthermore,

I wanted to ensure that all the areas would fill the rectangle and not spill outside. These constraints, and the variable depth of tree structures, challenged me for months until the sudden 'Aha!' moment hit me while in the faculty coffee room at the Department of Computer Science, University of Maryland.

It hadn't struck me, until then, that my computer and my phone and my tablet, all of these were structured like a tree—'branches of knowledge', that phrase was telling. Files as leaves, folders as branches, all these together made my computer a tree. Perhaps I ought to feel less guilty about spending time at the computer—after all, I am only spending time climbing a tree.

As I turned the pages of Lima's book to see how Western civilization had thought of every kind of structure—social, biological, religious, political, scientific, technological—in terms of the tree diagram, it had suppressed and denied something to the tree: its unpredictability. To be more precise, it was the geometry of unpredictability—the tree was expected to grow branches at certain intervals, alternating between right and left, and always in a linear fashion, never curving on itself or refusing to grow. The tree diagram demanded linear conformity—it worshipped structure. And so my doubts began to grow—this wasn't the kind of tree I wanted to be. Gilles Deleuze and Félix Guattari, the rarest kind of philosophers who wrote philosophy by tuning it to the stichomythic rhythm of poetry, had critiqued the tree model in their famous book *A Thousand Plateaus: Capitalism and Schizophrenia*, blaming the many follies of Western culture on it. Even before I read Deleuze and Guattari in my early twenties, I was aware of my unease with the tree diagram. It had come to me during a lecture on Bangla literature in high school. In an embarrassingly over-strung introductory lecture on the Tagores and their contribution to Bengali culture, our Bangla teacher, an otherwise brilliant woman who sometimes fell asleep in class, drew the Tagore 'family tree' and then asked us to draw ours. My parents had raised my brother and me without any sense of family history—we had no famous or even infamous ancestors. I could only go back one generation: to the names of my paternal and maternal grandparents; about their siblings or cousins I had neither any clue nor any active interest. So my 'family tree' looked nothing like a tree. It resembled, for all purposes, a cactus in a comic strip.

A Thousand Plateaus has a line that the philosophers, I had come to believe, had written specifically, if not only, for me: 'What if one became animal or plant *through* literature, which certainly does not become literarily?' That was what I had been doing for years now—looking for tree-shaped snug fits in that beanbag called literature. Lima thinks it is only 'normal that human beings, observing their intricate branching schemas and the seasonal withering and revival of their foliage, would see trees as powerful images of growth, decay, and resurrection. The veneration of trees, known as dendolatry, is tied to ideas of fertility, immortality, and rebirth and often is expressed by the axis mundi (world axis), world tree, or arbour vitae (tree of life)'. Lima runs the reader through a fascinating list—of the sacred Tooba tree from the Quran, the Yggdrasil, a huge ash tree that binds earth, hell and heaven together, of paintings, frescoes, sculptures of the Tree of Life, The Fall of Man, the tablet of the cross, the Mahabodhi Tree, the marriage of Shiva and Parvati under a sacred tree, the Tsonghapa refuge-host-field tree, Van Gogh's mulberry tree, Gustav Klimt's *The Tree of Life* with its convoluted ecosystem of animals, birds and fruits, and so on. More fascinating are the trees of the mind—'throughout human history the tree structure has been used to explain every facet of life: from consanguinity ties to cardinal virtues, systems of law to domains of science, biological associations to database systems. It has been such a successful model for graphically displaying relationships because it pragmatically expresses the materialization of multiplicity.'

'A first type of book is the root-book', write Deleuze and Guattari. 'The tree is already the image of the world, or the root the image of the world-tree. This is the classical book, as noble, signifying... the book imitates the world, as art imitates nature... Nature doesn't work that way: in nature, roots and taproots with a more multiple, lateral, and circular system of ramification, rather than a dichotomous one.' I knew, intuitively, that I didn't want to be this kind of tree. Anything with the word 'world' in it was fearsome to me: 'world-tree' was a monster. It doesn't end there. 'Many people have a tree growing in their heads, but the brain itself is much more like a grass than a tree,' they continue. This was about me—my right hand reached out to my head, to where it thought the brain was. 'Mathaye gachh gojiyechhey', a tree has grown out of your head, my mother's words, a scolding for being overtly imaginative, or when I mistakenly swallowed orange pips.

It is odd how the tree has dominated Western reality and all of Western thought, from botany to biology and anatomy, but also gnosiology, theology, ontology, all of philosophy...the root-foundation, Grund, racine, fondement. The West has a special relation to the forest, and deforestation; the fields carved from the forest are populated with seed plants produced by cultivation based on species lineages of the arborescent type... The East presents a different figure: a relation to the steppe and the garden (or in some cases, the desert and the oasis), rather than forest or field; cultivation of tubers by fragmentation of the individual... The West: agriculture based on a chosen lineage containing a large number of variable individuals. The East: horticulture based on a small number of individuals derived from a wide range of 'clones'. Does not the East, Oceania in particular, offer something like a rhizomatic model opposed in every respect to the Western model of the tree? Andre Haudricourt even sees this as the basis for the opposition between the moralities or philosophies of transcendence dear to the West and the immanent ones of the East: the God who sows and reaps, as opposed to the God who replants and unearths (replanting of offshoots versus sowing of seeds)... A rhizome has no beginning or end; it is always in the middle, between things, interbeing, intermezzo. The tree is filiation, but the rhizome is alliance, uniquely alliance. The tree imposes the verb 'to be', but the fabric of the rhizome is the conjunction, 'and...and...and...' This conjunction carries enough force to shake and uproot the verb 'to be'.

It is a brilliant passage, a manifesto to claim another way of looking and living, but after reading it a few times, I was left with the burden of wondering why I hadn't encountered a single memorable painting or sculpture of a ginger. That, and something else. If we had outsourced our entire thinking methodology to the branched system of trees, why was there no consciousness of *being* a tree? All the emoticons inside our phones and electronic devices use human faces—a semicolon followed by a closing bracket, for instance, is a cure to many tiffs. In spite of the tree image which humans have used to illustrate every possible situation or event in their lives, there is no emoticon—no tree image—that I could use to say that I feel like a tree.

TREE SCULPTURE

It is only now that I find myself wondering how I never posed as a tree when I played the game of 'Go Statue' as a child. In this childhood game, where someone counts backwards and the rest have to become statues as soon as the counting stops, my friends and I inevitably stood in the manner of the statues of Mahatma Gandhi, Subhas Chandra Bose and Benoy-Badal-Dinesh we had seen. Sometimes, we even allowed ourselves to mimic the peculiar mannerisms of our parents and teachers, poses by which they were identifiable to people: fathers returning from the market with heavy shopping bags, the hands of mothers stirring curries, the peon at school ringing the bell, teachers writing on blackboards, students singing the national anthem with their eyes tightly shut, such generic gestures.

Why is it that none of us ever posed as a tree statue? One of the reasons could be that the game gave children, otherwise powerless, the power to freeze motion, the same effect that the words of their parents and teachers had on them when they were up to some mischief. And so the freeze into statues of responsible adults as soon as the counting lapsed from child-time to adult-time. Seen from this perspective, which child would want to be a tree? Because of its immobility, a tree is already a statue. A tree statue would be a piece of tautology, frozen immobility, perhaps even an oxymoron.

After we built a house, I, at last, felt ready to provide a home to a few statues of trees, they of varying sizes and materials. A few days into the search, I realized that there were none to be bought—not in stone, not in brass, not in wood. And so, I began to pick up large dead trees from the roadside, ferrying them home on cycle rickshaws and vans, and picking up dead branches from visits to protected forests. I had grown exhausted of the sculptures of men, both of rulers and the ruled. I wanted more natural sculpture, where men had had little or no role to play in their design. Tree sculpture, branches nailed at angles to resemble abstract human and animal forms, sold at handicraft fairs. The shapes and the craftsman's instinct that had shaped them made me aware of what the artists had wanted to see in these amputated branches. Their surgery, through nails and glue, was not to give life to the branches but to the limbs in their mind.

This was some years before Subodh Gupta, one of India's most famous sculptors, created *Dada*, a banyan tree installation made of steel leaves and branches. Buckets, pots, pans, bowls, glasses, urns and pans, the props of modern kitchen life—these had been turned into banyan leaves in Gupta's sculpture. The utensils that stored food were stand-ins for leaves, the greatest food factory in the world. I saw it in photographs, the giant steel tree, its smooth surface glittering in the sun, the kind of tree that no one had ever seen.

But someone had imagined this steel tree before Subodh Gupta.

Wet almond-trees, in the rain,
Like iron sticking grimly out of earth;
Black almond trunks, in the rain,
Like iron implements twisted, hideous, out of the earth,
Out of the deep, soft fledge of Sicilian winter-green,
Earth-grass uneatable,
Almond trunks curving blackly, iron-dark, climbing the slopes.

Almond-tree, beneath the terrace rail,
Black, rusted, iron trunk,
You have welded your thin stems finer,
Like steel, like sensitive steel in the air,
Grey, lavender, sensitive steel, curving thinly and brittly up in a parabola.

What are you doing in the December rain?
Have you a strange electric sensitiveness in your steel tips?
Do you feel the air for electric influences

Like some strange magnetic apparatus?
Do you take in messages, in some strange code,
From heaven's wolfish, wandering electricity, that prowls so
constantly around Etna?
Do you take the whisper of sulphur from the air?

Do you hear the chemical accents of the sun?
Do you telephone the roar of the waters over the earth?
And from all this, do you make calculations?

Sicily, December's Sicily in a mass of rain
With iron branching blackly, rusted like old, twisted
implements
And brandishing and stooping over earth's wintry fledge,
climbing the slopes
Of uneatable soft green!

I had once learnt this poem by heart. I wanted to get inside D. H. Lawrence's mind, to see how he might have imagined a living tree as made of steel. It wasn't in 'Bare Almond Trees' alone—there seemed to be something about the almond tree that made it appear like iron to Lawrence. It was there in 'Almond Blossom' as well. 'The almond-tree, / December's bare iron hooks sticking out of earth.' These were tree sculptures like no other. As I read on, I discovered a kindred soul who worried about the violence wrought on trees—was it this that made him wish they were made of iron and steel? Why else that line, 'Like drawn blades never sheathed, hacked and gone black, the alien trees in alien lands'? Lawrence's trees have branches that could also be swords, to counter-attack the enemy if need be. And yet, in spite of the hardness of the iron—iron trees for an 'iron age'—the 'living steel' of the trees have 'the heart of blossom, / The unquenchable heart of blossom' in them.

Oh, honey-bodied beautiful one
Come forth from iron,
Red your heart is.

Is it only the instinct for self-preservation, then, that makes Lawrence imagine his trees as steel sculptures? Or is it the nature of sculpture itself, as something more permanent and lasting compared to the fickle destinies of trees that abet the train of thought?

The dead trees standing as sculpture in my house are perhaps my ways of retaining life's gait once the sap has stopped flowing, but why must the dead be denied a heart? A heart, I have begun to see, has no place in sculpture—blood is best invisible. That statues will not have hearts is a given. That tree statues won't have hearts is simply lazy tautology. And yet, Lawrence notices it, wants to see it. How many of us have ever gone to a statue to look for its heart?

It was difficult, after reading Lawrence, to not imagine a steel plate inside upright trees. When I saw photos of excavations, bones of dead animals arranged to resemble what their skeletons were when they were alive, I wondered why no archaeologist—or even botanist—had assembled a tree from its branches? The distinction would persist nevertheless, I was aware—the animal would become a specimen, a scientific prop, and the tree would, by some strange alchemy, turn into a piece of art. The tree 'skeleton', that structure that refused to make a distinction between the outside and the inside, the public and the private, would neither inspire awe nor fear.

At the bend was another wayward query. Could there be a nude tree? I've learned this from plants—there is no nudity at all. Death emphasized it in extravagance—our helpless nudity, both plants' and ours. In that every tree statue is a 'nude', a delightful and most innocent beauty.

Truth be told, I wasn't very eager to see 'living' statues of trees. *The Willowman Project*, headed by Axel Erlandson, had literally given arbour sculpture a new twist—a bean farmer by profession, Erlandson had grafted sycamore trees in various ways to produce what he called 'Circus Trees'. This made me uncomfortable, as extreme performances of the human body did in a circus or athletics competition. Bonsais, trees dwarfed by human hands, had never appealed to me for the same purpose—there was no beauty in such extreme human domination. For trees and their naturally sculpted bodies are as dependent on context as their produce is on soil and climatic conditions. The Japanese thinker

Tetsuro Watsuji noticed what he called the strangeness of 'Western trees' when he first saw them, standing erect and stoic, their bodies perpendicular to the earth. About the trees in Italy, the same place that gave birth to Lawrence's steel-tree poems, Watsuji writes, 'I realized that this feeling of artificiality arose from my being conditioned by the irregularities of tree shapes in my own surroundings; for, in Japan, such precision is the product only of man's hand. In Europe, however, the natural and regular go hand in hand; irregularity of form is unnatural. Whereas in Japan the artificial and rational go together, in Europe it is the natural that goes with the rational.' Italy, the heartland of the European Renaissance, with its manifesto of proportion and form, might owe its artistic life to a visual conditioning by its trees, who can tell.

PHOTOGRAPHING TREES

The family inside my head continues to grow. A photographer I discovered on the Internet by the name of Beth Moon had spent the last fourteen years of her life standing with a camera in front of what she calls 'ancient' trees. Moon's photos of these trees, some more than a thousand years old, one even older than four thousand, in her book *Ancient Trees: Portraits of Time*, came as a lesson. Moon calls these trees 'monuments'—it is a testimony to the history making capacities of plant life, and she calls these photographs 'portraits', a genre reserved for humans in the hierarchy of photographs. These photographs, in grey, black and sepia, use a nineteenth-century technology of printing, a choice Beth Moon found compatible with the subject she was dealing with—the passage of time unannotated by rush or speed. The photographs of these ancient trees spread across continents, give us an alternative history of the planet and, of course, a new understanding of monuments as being living and statuesque at the same time. Beth Moon's time-lapse photos of trees also make us aware of slow time in a way which our tight human notions of beginnings and ends can't.

When I'd first begun writing about plant life, I'd noticed a change in the way I wrote, not immediately, but possibly after a few months. I remember the sudden change in the rhythm of my breathing. Speed, choking, stifling, bruising speed—my body and my mind could not run to machine time anymore. The concept of the tortuous deadline no longer mattered to me, the psychological gestures, postures and traumas associated with living to calendar time also disappeared when I sat down to think—and later, write—about trees. I began to look forward to that time of writing in a therapeutic way—not in the way one thinks of writing a book or finishing a project but as something I didn't want ever to end.

As I have said at the outset, in wanting to become a tree, I had, without realizing it, begun to live to 'tree time'. An hour or two every day, often less, given my work-cramped life, but it was a drug like no other: I gradually began to get addicted to this bubble of slow time. It began to show in the tentativeness of my sentences too—I sensed a growing unease with punctuation marks, and definitely with units like paragraphs. They seemed too presumptuous, too artificial for tree language. Was it possible to write like a tree? I was concerned too that this part-time living to tree time would make me lose my sense of grammar for that is what my understanding of grammar was—a linguistic baton with which to control time. Tree time, with its expansive caesuras, would surely seem too leisurely to post-industrial humans—Beth Moon's photos had used time lapse to condense moments of process into points of effect. I use the word 'effect' with caution because I am not sure whether there really is an 'effect' that trees aim for.

The primary reason why Beth Moon's photographs appealed to me was because Moon had worked to tree time. Slow time is not laziness—who would be foolish enough to call a plant lazy? Trees and humans share the diurnal pattern of time, of working and inactivity, but time for man had, at some point, begun speeding up, and the difference began to grow.

My need to become a tree, then, was a need to return to slow time.

Part III

See the Long Shadow that is Cast by the Tree?
— Czesław Miłosz, '*Faith*'

PORTRAIT OF A TREE

Like many, I too once desired a painter as lover. The alchemy of love—adolescence pampers the notion of love as chemistry—would rid me of my imperfections and his portrait of me would make me beautiful to him and to myself. When I began drawing leaves I began to wonder whether such an impulse would attend this love. If I were a tree—and I hoped and believed I was turning into one—would a painter lover feel the urge, or even the need, to turn me into something else, someone else? For what is beauty and perfection in trees? I turned to the man I had married. He had been an amateur painter once. Only three drawings survived from that period in his life: two were portraits of women, copied, as he explained to me, from a magazine that was common in Bengali households: *Soviet Nari*. He had been taken by the beauty of two women in those hormone-rushed teenage years and thought this the only way to create a relationship with them. The other painting still hangs on a wall in our living room. In it is a tree trunk with many branches. From a distance it might look like a many-handed goddess, as it first did to me when I visited this house for the first time one winter afternoon more than two decades ago. This rectangular canvas has less tree and more shadows in it. One must guess the shape of the branches above from the shadows scattered on the ground. It has the likeness of a game. Before we got married, in one of those moments in which we tried to act like the adults we wanted to be in the future, I asked him about the painting. I did not consider it special, but it was his way of looking at something I loved, and I wanted to be made aware of how he looked at it. It was one of the most difficult portraits he had drawn, he said, and when I asked him why, his answer made me look at the painting in a completely different way. It had taken him days to get the correct proportion of shadows of the branches of the tree. From those shadows a viewer could guess the time of the day, perhaps even the season. But it wasn't that which interested me. In my future husband's gaze at the tree I wanted to find a clue to his way of looking at the world. He might as well have been looking at a woman, and in that gaze I wanted to find an estimate of his world view. All I wanted to know was whether he thought the tree an equal. And so his use of the word 'portrait' came as a happy surprise to me. For who had ever heard of tree portraits? Weren't they reserved for men?

A BRIEF HISTORY OF SHADOWS

That there is no history of shadows is one of the saddest absences in our archives. In that laziness is also the refusal to see any worth in the transient, the old privileging of, say, a romantic 'forever' over the 'affair'. Shadows are affairs, short-lived and short-sighted ones. I have, in moments of heat-and-light-exhaustion, allowed myself to think of a state—a State perhaps?—where shadows are illegal. What would one do in such a place then? Imagine carrying a pair of scissors with you always, trying to cut your shadow from yourself, that dark creature trailing you from behind or sideways. I say all this because a long time ago, when I was little, I had that overwhelming sense of shadows being trespassers.

I was wandering through a mango orchard in Malda, a district in Bengal famous for the fruit. The estate belonged to a friend of my grandfather's and my father and uncles had brought their children there for a picnic. A game was devised immediately: Collect Mangoes. The person with the highest number of mangoes would be given a 'prize'. The only condition was that we were only allowed to collect mangoes from the ground. A younger cousin was caught cheating—he had climbed on to an old and giving mango tree. By the end of the afternoon, all of us, eleven children, had mangoes in varying stages of ripeness. A few of us had not been able to resist the temptation of biting into the fruits. The greed and its consequences showed around their sap-sticky mouths. We stood in a queue like well-behaved children expecting rewards. I was the oldest at nine, also the tallest. Obeying rules of queuing learned at school, I stood right at the end, the basket in my hand covered shyly—even slyly—with my hanky. I heard adult words of full-throated praise for the mango-picking abilities of all of us children. My nervousness increased when it came to my turn to show off the mangoes I had collected.

My basket was empty.

My uncles looked at me with pity, the kind that comes naturally for their intelligent eldest brother's stupid firstborn. From the corner of my right eye I could see my father's moustache—it looked angry to me. I knew the first word that would ring out when I got home.

My favourite uncle, always quick to take my side, said, 'Such a sacrificing elder sister she is. She must have given her mangoes to the younger lot.'

I shook my head. I hadn't. 'I was collecting shadows of mangoes,' I said. 'And now they are all gone.'

They laughed together but did not understand why I had wanted to find out whether shadows could be collected. Instead they turned my experiment into a fable: are shadows of sweet fruits sweet too?

Now, nearly three decades later, I cannot remember—or even imagine—what made me want to collect mango shadows instead of mangoes. What I do remember is walking through the orchard and suddenly feeling burdened by the weight of the tree shadows that had fallen on me. Perhaps it was that that had made me want to take revenge on these trees by collecting the shadows of their fruits? Would that have made the trees feel bereft? Perhaps no more than tearing fruits from them would have done, but how could I have known?

For months—or was it weeks?—I would see what I considered the underside of the shadows of trees in my sleep. I would gather words to tell my mother about this harassment from tree shadows, but when morning came, only the fear would remain, the images would be gone just like shadows do in the invading dark.

Because all of us can't climb trees the shadows of trees fall to the ground was one of the things that occurred to me at the time. I hadn't learned to climb trees then and this was the closest that I could get to the experience—by stamping on the shadows of branches I could simulate climbing. But the teeth-like edges of the tops of trees scared me and I wished their tops were plateaus instead of sharp mounds.

It is for doctors to diagnose why I continued to be obsessed with

Sumana Roy

the shadows of trees. I now remember, with much embarrassment, my parents being summoned for 'discussions' in school. On one occasion, I refused to enter the playground and screamed when the ayahs forced me to. The reason was a grapefruit tree standing guard at the entrance. The tree looked like an exhausted Atlas to me, carrying so many Earths on its shoulder. In my mind, the heavy shadows of the tree's plump fruits looked so burdensome that it seemed they could be wrenched off their stalks at any moment. What if the shadows of obese grapefruits fell on my head?

Like most parents who are compelled to practise patience in order to survive child-rearing, my parents gritted their teeth and waited for my fancies to subside. One winter picnic to Kalijhora, a picturesque spot on the banks of the river Teesta, I began screaming. At first they thought it was motion sickness, but a little investigation by my annoyed father revealed that I had begun to imagine the shadows of trees by the side of the road as three-dimensional. Imagine the number of accidents that would take place if shadows were material things—would we have planted trees by the roadside then?

I now wonder whether all this was intentional on my part.

I wish I could remember.

All I can remember of those tree shadows now is the scolding of my art teacher—'Why are your umbrellas always tree shaped?'

When I first began thinking seriously—the right word would be 'painfully'—about shadows, the first writer I wanted to read was Roy Sorensen. The name of his extraordinary book is *Seeing Dark Things: The Philosophy of Shadows*. By the time I had come to the eighth page of his book, Sorensen was putting into words the intuitive connections I had once made while trying to differentiate the falling of leaves from the fall of shadows from a tree:

> Deciduous trees practice similar indirection. They are designed to shed leaves with the approach of cold weather. But they actually shed leaves in accordance with the declining length of the days. Consequently, the trees drop leaves even in an unseasonably

warm autumn and do not adjust their schedule to the early onset of cold weather. Just as it is easier for the tree to measure daylight than temperature, it is easier for the relevant module of the visual system to measure the orientation of an object relative to the retina.

Sorensen had understood the psychosomatic orientation of the tree, its prioritizing light over temperature, and therein its distinction from humans. But I wanted to know more—did the tree care as much for its falling shadows as it did for its fallen leaves? If there had been no gravity, would the tree shadows have fallen to the earth at all? I was aware of the independence of shadows from gravity, and yet, in a moment of fantasy, I wondered how it would feel to see shadows stuck in midair, like trapeze artists soaring from one end of the circus tent to the other, never falling except in a cruel accident. What if tree shadows—or shadows in general—fell to earth only by accident?

There was something else that I could not have not noticed—how the human imagination had turned both fallen leaves and falling shadows into art. For fall, a name that had come from the falling of leaves in the season, was also a minor subgenre of painting and photography. Beginning late September, my Facebook newsfeed was filled with photos of leaves and shadows in varying stages of 'fall', as the colloquial expression went.

What fascinated me most were tree silhouettes, those half-shadow creatures that indulged the imagination to think of terrifying monsters and fantastic centaurs. 'Shadows are far stranger than silhouettes. Shadows are not parts of their material casters. They must be caused by material things but can (briefly) survive the destruction of their casters,' writes Sorensen. I now remember, with near equal delight and embarrassment, the shadow plays of my childhood in 1980s Bengal during power cuts, also called load-shedding to give it gravitas and poetry, and the different permutations of our fingers in front of the kerosene lamps and candles. Deer and rabbit and frog and reindeer and fish and helicopter. My mother, always an enthusiast for the games children played, recited a Bangla poem in our dark living room one day.

Aek je chhilo gachh
Shondhey holay du haat tuley jurto bhooter naach...

Once upon a time there was a tree
As soon as evening fell, it raised its hands and began the ghost
dance...

The tree immediately became a ghost in our minds, and in spite of
the fear of the invisible suddenly turning visible, which is where my
childhood fear of ghosts lay, I found that suddenly all of us wanted to
become ferocious tree shadows. We began collecting dried twigs and
branches for the next installment of the light-and-shadow drama, a
playmate even brought firewood. We were united in our ambition to
produce cruel and terrifying trees. And yet, when my mother's grades
for our performance as trees arrived, none of us who used dead tree
parts won. It was the lanky Debu who impressed my mother the most.
This he owed to his yoga teacher Bappa-da—the man had taught him
vrikshasana, the human body becoming a tree. His right leg was bent
into a triangle, the foot resting on the side of his left knee, his hands
folded into a namaskar above his head. I was angry with my mother's
judgement for I had never seen a tree like that in my life. When I later
complained to her, she said that all of us, not Debu alone, had also been
making shadow figures of imaginary trees.

Our fascination with shadows, I learnt, begins in infancy, and so
I began to pester my mother for stories about that period in my life.
And questions: are trees scared of the dark? Are baby trees more scared
of the dark than adult trees? But our relationship with shadows is
so unimportant to our memory-making that no one remembers it,
not even mothers who remember childhood falls and punishments
in school. Since no answers were forthcoming from my mother, I
began to focus on my nephew's relationship with tree shadows. On his
second Christmas, when he was about fifteen months old, my father
got a Christmas tree for the toddler. It stood beside his bed, by the
window, where it obstructed the sun's invasion. One morning, my
mother discovered the baby licking the shadow of the pointy top of
the tree on the bedcover. The shadow looked like an ice cream cone,

at least to our adult imagination, but the little boy had never seen or tasted anything like an ice cream cone before. 'Children are much slower to acquire a comparable understanding of shadows,' writes Sorensen. Was that why the shadow of the Christmas tree had become an edible thing to my little nephew?

❦

Though I thought nothing of it then, I now realize that my relationship with trees came to be inevitably mediated through its shadows. The day I came to know, for instance, that there were no shadows at noon, I was outraged—for me that was the equivalent of cutting a tree. My school friends continue to tease me about the impassioned Class Six essay I wrote on the subject: can one kill a tree by killing its shadow? Some other thoughts on shadows, and their relationship to trees. Of all living things, it is trees that are most unconcerned about their shadows. Other things being equal, trees don't need to be careful of treading on shadows like others need to. Take the case of Alexander's horse:

> King Philip of Macedon refused to buy a beautiful horse named Bucephalus. None of his grooms could control the beast. His ten-year-old son Alexander then asked to try his skill. Although fearing for his son's safety, King Philip reluctantly agreed. The prince turned the agitated horse to face the sun—Alexander had noticed that Bucephalus was frightened by his shadow. Calmed, the horse obediently showed off his paces, to the loud applause of the court. Philip kissed his son and said, 'Seek another kingdom that may be worthy of your abilities, for Macedonia is too small for you.'

As I read this in Sorensen, I wondered how the story might have played out had Bucephalus been a tree and not a horse. Imagine a tree—or a group of 'mentally disturbed' trees—troubled by its own shadow and throwing a scare-induced tantrum every time it spotted its shadow.

❦

When I walked along pavements and thoroughfares, with the shade of trees guarding me from the harsh sun, I would encounter various signs asking for better civic behaviour: do not throw things on the road, instructions about stray animals, and so on. Tree shadows were also thrown on the road, but alone among the other things that littered the roadside, these were a welcome presence. After sundown, when I returned by the same route and found them missing, I was filled with sadness—but it was only temporary. For I knew they would be there the next morning. Another thought upon seeing a tree shadow: even if the tree is unfamiliar, shadows are always comfortable and familiar. For the shadows of trees obliterate specificity, the colour of bark and leaves and flower and fruit. Just like the shadows of humans do not reflect race, class, or religion.

X-RAYING PLANTS

I remember a visit to a national park where our guide, who had so far been telling us about the animals, stopped to point to a Goliath-sized tree. The annual examination results in school had been declared the previous day—this trip was my father's gift to me. I was now in Class Eight. My father had said to me when I entered my new grade that I was almost an adult, and what I did or did not do now would become most apparent when I was old. I remember being happy to be considered an adult, but I did not look forward to being old. The old were worse than children—they had nothing to look forward to, I was convinced. So when the guide told us, in a voice reserved for inciting awe in listeners, that this tree was more than two hundred years old, I saw the eyes of fellow tourists scale the height of the tree and then measure its girth. The guide was clever and observant. He noticed that I was looking not at the tree but for something around it.

'This tree has no flowers for you to pick,' he told me.

'I am not looking for flowers,' I said.

'No edible fruits either,' he clarified.

I did not reply. As I was now an adult, I had recently discovered—how could I have told him about what adults, led by my parents, thought an abnormality?

In the end, I succumbed: 'If this tree is more than two centuries old, its shadows of two hundred years must have accumulated here. Where is the sediment of its shadows?'

Much later, the truth would come to me during one of my feverish shadow hunting expeditions as an adult, sometimes armed with a camera. Though a forest is a luxury home for trees, there are very few tree shadows to be found in it. This is another piece of truth about these shadows—their beauty is a celebration of individualism. Smaller tree shadows are absorbed—hidden—behind larger trees. That also explains why tree parasites, usually small, have been denied the right to cast shadows.

It wasn't as though I had discovered the beauty of shadows from the get go. In the beginning I was terrified of them. Their seeming scariness was exacerbated because of my fear of the dark. For a time I was also fearful about shadows because I felt there was something about them that was paranormal, that they were hiding something that was monstrous. Perhaps this had something to do with an incident from my childhood. Looking for censored reading material when alone at home due to a forced convalescence after a long illness, this when I was in Class Six, I discovered, among other tiny books and curious images, a box of photographic negatives. With sweaty palms and an oxidized imagination, I rummaged through the stack hungrily. It seemed to me, though I could never be sure, that the people in these negatives were my parents. At first I was angry with them for having hidden this past life from me, this life, which my teenage imagination promptly decided, had to do with making me. The man in the trousers and the woman in the sari, the white spaces of the clothes in the negatives, looked close, even intimate, in a way I'd never seen my parents. I wanted to discover more, but soon a fear took root. This wasn't about being discovered by my parents, but something else. In all the photographic negatives, there were monstrous looking creatures in the background. I suddenly remembered my mother telling me about her joyful trips to the Botanical Gardens in Shibpur with my father, when both of them were students with meagre pocket money. Was it this then, my parents as Adam and Eve in these negatives? The physical proximity between their bodies, visually exaggerated by the white spaces in the negatives, looked terribly in need of censure.

That night I could not sleep. The first installment of fear, propelled by their discovery of my discovery, was gone. I had erred, but given the state of my health, I knew my parents would not punish me with any degree of severity. However, whenever I closed my eyes, those monsters in the background moved out of my head into the tiny dark bedroom so that it seemed like I was being swallowed by black and white octopus arms. Long after midnight, when fear had left me exhausted, I realized what these monsters were—the negatives of the ancient trees of the Botanical Gardens.

The character of fear being what it is, my fascination with these tree figures did not cease. I began pestering a radiologist friend to help me take X-rays of my favourite plants. I say plants because it was impossible for him to take the heavy X-ray machine outdoors to investigate the inner lives of trees. On Saturday evenings I would enter the diagnostic clinic with a large bag. Inside it would be a plant in a pot. My friend would wait for everyone else to leave the clinic for the weekend. And then the pot would be placed in exactly the same position where my chest might have been, had it been my X-ray that he wanted to take. This continued for weeks until both his niceness and my curiosity began to wither. Perhaps this was the only way to get plants to reveal their 'inner lives' to me. I suppose I'd longed for these X-ray films to be the equivalent of memoirs, art distilling the lived life into a pleasurable art form. But it did not work out that way and my curiosity faded.

Two things happened recently that reawakened my interest in X-rays of trees. One was an old news report that a friend forwarded me: X-ray photographer Nick Veasey had, in 2011, taken an X-ray photo of a Christmas tree along with all the Christmas gifts placed under it. For most, the excitement lay in the 'hidden' surprises made visible, but my thrill was in watching the X-ray photo of the Christmas tree, with the geometry of its decorations hanging from it. For a moment it made me wonder retrospectively how an X-ray photographer might have shot me in my wedding finery. This was a 'special occasion' photograph, and unlike the millions of photos of Christmas trees inside homes and in public places, there was something touchingly intimate about it—with the bling and glitter of the gifts and decorations gone, the X-ray had been able to capture every minute bend and twirl of the pine leaves. In my mind it was the closest a human could get to tree art.

Technology altered my gaze as well: I bought an iPad and discovered the X-ray photo option in its 'photo booth'. As I dabbled

Sumana Roy

with X-ray photos I became momentarily interested only in the tree's relationship with darkness and light. I, who had spent so much energy debating about the lack of the real act of people eating in paintings and photographs, became temporarily obsessed with wanting to capture plants in the process of eating. But what did plants eat? Light, of course. Of all human acts of eating, it was gluttony that interested me the most—it was a tragicomic genre, my favourite. I wanted to shoot gluttonous trees, overfeeding on light. Where would I find such a moment, this surfeit of light? At last it came to me: lightning. I would capture trees feeding on lightning in the darkness. I imagined it as the trees' version of the midnight feast.

I was only an amateur photographer, and had comfortably spent most of my life in auto mode. How was I to turn this act of midnight gluttony into something resembling art? There was also something else—the unpredictable nature of lightning. One never knew, in spite of all the theoretical knowledge available, when a bolt of lightning might strike, and most importantly where one might fall. Another thought had not struck me until almost the last moment. Much as I wanted to be a tree, live like a tree, one of the insurmountable hurdles I faced was sexual violence. The chances of a tree being struck by lightning were far lower than that of a woman being raped if she was out alone in the dark. Disappointed, I turned to scavenging photographs of trees against the background of lightning. This over long hours, days, then weeks, until I was overcome with nausea, the kind that must be the consequence of gluttony.

In most of these photographs, the trees looked scared and timid, at least to my imagination. They had once looked beautiful to me— the extraordinary voltage of light and darkness, the faux classicism of natural sepia, a tinged black and white as it were, the outstretched branches of the dark tree provoking the kind of hormone that brings business to horror films. But now, that was all gone. In its stead was an overwhelming nausea of a kind I'd felt once after looking at photos of poverty pornography, photos in which a photographer friend had made the slums of a suburb look 'beautiful'.

The reaction of trees to light moved me in numberless ways. I longed for that noiselessness of consumption that marked their relationship. No one liked noisy eaters and I was no exception. It was beautiful, this soundless eating of light by trees. Were shadows their excretory products then?

But it was not sound but sight that had drawn me to these shadows. Sitting under a tree one day, my shadow having merged with the shadow of the tree so that an overhead observer of the shadow would not have been able to spot a human leaning against the tree trunk, I wondered why no culture had ever turned a tree shadow into an iconographic symbol. A shadow is only a hole made in the light, and for months I experimented with the holes that my plants made: the head of a cactus when put in front of a table lamp in a dark room became a pincushion on a wall; shadows of grass on a moving white sari screen began resembling a giant army of foot soldiers marching to war; and because light does not make a distinction between the big and the small, even fleshy-stemmed wandering Jew plants in pots threw giant shadows on the wall that made them look more like an autonomous colony than any banyan I have seen. The experiments still continue though the enthusiasm has slackened. This is because I have come to realize that I was guilty of the same urge as most tree shadow enthusiasts: we allow the tree shadow to become an animal or thing or monster, but very rarely, or almost never, do we imagine the shadows of other objects or animals as trees.

In Class Seven, at the end of the academic year, our science teacher made us write, anonymously, about one scientific invention that we would like to see made possible in our lifetime. I think he might have used the anonymity trick to help us overcome our shyness—he was one of the finest teachers a young student could have, a rare breed of science teacher who made us partners in the great provocation that science is. Many of my friends, hungry teenagers as we were, wanted scientists to invent instant food supplying machines: think of chocolates, and lo, the next moment they would be in your mouth. My wish was a little different: 'I wish for a machine that would help me recognize people and trees from their shadows.' When I got married, this teacher gave me a drawing book of handmade paper. On the third page was the inscription—'May you continue to be a psychologist of shadows.' All these years he had known that it was me who had written that anonymous wish.

'Only I can cast my shadow,' says Sorensen. By that logic, no two tree shadows should be the same. This is a piece of truth we know and do not know. For who has ever cared to find out? We love to inhabit theories that tell us that there are exactly seven people on this planet who resemble each other completely. In spite of my affection for trees, I have never cared to find out likenesses for shadows of plants and trees I have loved. Behind this notion of the individualism of trees is my curious question—even if two trees are not alike can't their two shadows be alike? For in this was ambition: I might not be a tree, but couldn't my shadow be tree-shaped?

FEEDING LIGHT TO TREES

How do you actually feed light to trees? The Bangla phrase for putting house plants outdoors is literally that—rode khawano, feeding them sunlight. I had had my experiments with trees as light gluts, but the pain of watching LEDs and fairy lights bandaged around trees to make them statues of light was unbearable. Loving ice cream is one thing but being made to swim naked in a bathtub of ice cream is another. How long can one eat? How could the trees tolerate this, this surfeit of light? The unnaturalness of this was made plain to me by the winged creatures: no bird ever sat on an electrically-lit tree. When I mentioned this to a friend who had been posting effervescent photos of such trees from a park in New York on Facebook, her reply was the standard: 'There are greater offences than this.' The need for beauty to the human eye involves, without a doubt, the most violent of processes—threading, waxing, cosmetic surgery, the like. Trees had not been exempted. The bare trees of December, whom I imagined in great need of leaves, their kitchens, were not beautiful enough— electric lights would turn them into burning brides. Whatever you imagined them to be. But in spite of the light, these trees, with LED strings taped to their bodies, did not cast shadows.

The art—temporary, fleeting and sunlight dependent art—created by tree shadows was, in my mind, a kind of Art Brut, raw art, or what has been called 'Outsider Art', art created by the untrained, the self-taught. For about this I was certain—my closest identification with trees came from the fact that both of us were autodidacts.

BECOMING A SHADOW

In the evening, I let my shadow out on the field—there my limbs and its shadows worked to their own logic and on a few lucky days, when the angle and light and everything else fell into a synchronic alliance, I saw my shadow turning into a tree, a tree with branches, a tree waiting for leaves.

I had still not managed to become a tree. But I had at least become its shadow.

Part IV

Supposing I Became a Champa Flower
—Rabindranath Tagore, '*The Champa Flower*'

RABINDRANATH TAGORE'S GARDEN

Subarnarekha, a bookshop, is a kind of parallel institution in Bengal's Bolpur, where Visva-Bharati, the university founded by Rabindranath Tagore, is situated. Located at the mouth of the street that brings students, professors and visitors from the archives in Rabindra Bhavan, it is a rich source of second-hand gossip and anecdotes about books and people in Santiniketan.

I had come specifically for stories about the trees that I saw around me, their scientific names nailed to their bodies on tin plates. But when have you ever heard gossip about plant life? For days I waited impatiently, bugging the young owner for *anything* that would tell me more about the trees here—I'd been persuaded by stories of their foreignness to come here. On the fourth day, as I sat perched on the low staircase that leads to the bookshop, the owner gave me a consoling smile. I followed him like a tendril around a stout pole. It was a photocopy of *Trees of Santiniketan*: he had copied the cover page too, and I found myself touching the sad flatness of the photocopied image. For some reason, I imagined the cover art by Surendranath De richer than it might have been—it was, after all, only a painting of a generic knotted tree with stylized tiny leaves.

It must have been a lucky day for me for that morning in Rabindra Bhavan's book section, I had discovered and then bought a thin book in Bangla. Entitled *Uttarayan-er Bagaan O Gachhpala* (The Garden and Trees of Uttarayan), it was written by Debiprosonno Chattopadhyay. Uttarayan is the collective name given to the five houses—Konark, Shyamali, Punoshcho, Udichi, and Chitrovanu—where Rabindranath spent most of his last years, and Chattopadhyay gives us a brief history about the dwelling places of the Tagores. The garden at Uttarayan was created between 1919 and 1938. In these two decades, Rabindranath's son, Rathindranath, who had been sent to America to study the agricultural sciences, structured the five houses along with their adjoining gardens, courtyards and tree spaces in a manner that could be said to stand as living evidence of what 'Visvabharati' meant and stood for—the world and Bharat, India. For the Rajasthani and Buddhist and Islamic influences on the architecture of Uttarayan were counterbalanced by the Italian, English, Japanese and Chinese gardens that Rathindranath and his talented and curious wife, Protima Debi, happened to see on their travels abroad or hear in stories from Rabindranath himself.

Debiprosonno Chattopadhyay spent his work life of nearly four decades in these gardens. Having joined as caretaker of the gardens in 1963, when Protima Debi was still alive, he began writing his book in 1997, close to the time of his retirement. Having spent the first six years of his professional life under the tutelage of Protima Debi, who passed away in 1969, Chattopadhyay was fed on stories about the inspiration and effort that moved Rathindranath to design such garden spaces. One particular ethic was passed down from Rabindranath to his son and then to the other caretakers after their death—it was that the gardens had to have a balance of plants in such a manner that there would be a crowd of flowering plants throughout the year, irrespective of season or the time of the year. Rathindranath brought botany and his love of aesthetics into this, true, but it was the independent life of trees there that gives Santiniketan so much of its beauty and character. This is to be seen, for instance, in the birth and later history of the shimool tree near 'Konark', the first of the Uttarayan houses. Rani Chanda, Rabindranath's caregiver in his last years, whose husband, Anil Chanda, was also the poet's secretary, writes about the famous shimool tree that is now associated with the house: 'A baby shimool sapling raised its head near the verandah opposite Konark. The sight made Gurudev happy. He began to look after it and watered it regularly. Rathi-da (Rathindranath) was scared because the shimool tree grows rather fast, and this one looked terribly feeble. It could topple over during a fierce windy storm, and then the verandah and its roof would come crumbling down too. It was better to not let the tree grow there. The thought, when it came to Gurudev, left him sad. The tree began to grow fiercely, its head climbing up a little with each day. One monsoon, a flowering climber, a *malotilata*, showed up below the tree. Gurudev wrapped the tender stem around the youthful shimool: let the weak stem find a little support and a home. That shimool turned into a grand old tree one day. The tender stems and tendrils of the *malotilata* continue to be wrapped around the tree.'

Rabindranath Tagore's father, Maharshi Debendranath, inaugurated this garden space by basing his place for meditation around two chhatim trees in 1863, when Rabindranath was two years old. He had chosen this place in Bolpur for its peoplelessness, but this largely uninhabited space was barren. He got the pebble-filled soil of Bolpur replaced with arable soil, an immense task that is difficult to imagine even after a hundred and fifty years. Soon mango, jackfruit, horitoki, jamun, coconut, sal, palm, weeping willows, bokul, the kadam and mahua trees began growing there. The name 'Santiniketan', the abode of peace, would come much later. This enterprise of turning barren land into an oasis filled with the best kind of tropical fruit bearing trees led the locals to give this place a new name. There was no need for poetry. They called it, simply, 'bagaan', garden. And that was how it all began.

More land was acquired, and the garden began to stretch and spill out onto new spaces, but Debendranath, austere and almost puritanical in his ways, stuck to the same place that had first brought him to Santiniketan—the shadow of the twin chhatim trees. This was mainly the handiwork of a gardener by the name of Ramdas. The journal, *Unity and Minister*, mentioned this man in particular in an essay, 'Pilgrimage Of Santiniketan Or Bolpur', in its 2 October 1901 issue: 'It is a noteworthy fact that the gardener by name of Ramdas [sic], who laid the Santiniketan Garden, had at first been to the employment of Raja Rammohun Roy who took him to England and after the death of the Master, he returned to India and was engaged by the Burdwan Maharaj to his famous "Golap Bag" Garden. The Maharshi whose taste in these matters is princely, had engaged this man for doing good work.'

When Rabindranath came to live in Santiniketan permanently in 1901, he set up his 'Brahmacharya' ashram close to where his father used to meditate, near the twin chhatim trees. Santiniketan began to grow gradually, and so did its tree spaces: Shaalbithi, the abode around the sal trees; Aamrokunjo, the room in the midst of the mango groves; Madhabikunjo, the house adjacent to the sweet smelling madhabi flowers.

I have often heard it said that the Tagores—on account of their contribution to culture, literature, music, the arts, culinary traditions, sartorial innovations, and so on—changed the way Bengalis live. I have never seen or heard anyone commending the way in which at least three generations of Tagores nurtured plant life in an inhospitable space.

My maternal grandparents, both of them doctors trained in England several years before India got Independence from the British, decided to settle in Bolpur's Bhubandanga a few years after 1947. Rathindranath was still alive—when he died, my grandmother, who'd known him briefly, made my mother plant a bougainvillea shrub in their backyard. My grandfather came from a family of landowners that had landed property in the districts of Birbhum and Burdwan in Bengal, but after taking his FRCS degree, he returned to Howrah, close to Calcutta, to practise medicine. My grandmother, an Englishwoman who had abandoned every robe and rag of familiarity to accompany her husband back to his homeland, was a textbook Orientalist. By the early 1950s she had tired of city life, or so she thought, and taken in by her own DIY version of back-to-nature, managed to convince my grandfather to 'follow', perhaps replicate, Rabindranath's journey. Tagore, the poet, was, for many of her generation, a pop philosopher who had managed to crack life's code, the true hippie before Woodstock, as it were. And so they came to Bolpur—a clay house was built immediately, and my grandmother took to this way of life with a vengeance. Poultry farming, keeping a cow, a kitchen garden, tree saplings collected from the Botanical Gardens in Calcutta's Shibpur, where they knew an officer—she did all this and more.

I did not know her—she died when I was less than a year old, and so my impression of her is formed of recollections of her from my mother, her brother and his wife, and my older cousins. She died a few years after Protima Debi, Rathindranath's wife and, in spite of age-related physical ailments, she took a walk every evening to the Uttarayan complex. My mother mentions some of the gardening habits she copied from the gardening staff at Visva-Bharati, but about one thing she remained completely unwavering—her refusal to fashion a 'proper' garden. She refused to believe that Rabindranath had actually cared for what she thought was the 'artificial' beauty of gardens.

Gardens are often settings in Tagore's short stories, novels and novellas, and Chattopadhyay reminds us that the poet was very impressed by Ahmedabad's Shahibag and the garden in his tutor Anna Tarkhar's house in Bombay. There is also the famous rose garden of Shilaidaha, where he spent his early life. But his admiration for such structures would have remained confined to his writing had his son Rathindranath, along with Surendranath Kar and Nandalal Bose, not fashioned his vision into living gardens.

Rabindranath's concern and affection for plants is revealed in the many letters he wrote to his daughters and friends, especially when he was away from Santiniketan. In the summer of 1933, for instance, he writes to his daughter Mira: 'At last my *madhumaloti* has acquired some health. Do not forget to cool her down with your bath water from now on. Ask them to plant neem, shirish, and other trees on the street that leads to my room this monsoon. It's not a bad idea to plant a few jackfruit trees either... The spire from the temple that's been broken, keep that in a corner of my garden and get the *jhumkolata* to climb on to it.'

Rabindranath's homesickness included missing his family of plants. From hilly Mungpoo in Darjeeling, he writes to Visva-Bharati employee Sachidananda Roy: 'Pay attention to the garden. A few chameli bushes need to be planted to give the name "Chamelia" some credibility. I love tall trees, but they shouldn't be very close to the house. Keep in mind the drumstick tree—it flowers in winter but is quick to grow tall. Mahaneem, shimool, these take root in the soil there quite easily...fences made out of the wild jui look lovely. Cows do not eat red oleanders, but the flowers have a kind of glory; white and red kawrobi should run parallel to each other. The fragrance of lemon flowers is a favourite, keep some provision for that. The flowers of the chalta tree have great flamboyance, shirish, jamrool, roses I like for their flowers. When Mahadeb is on leave, employ a hardworking gardener in his place. The gardens will need watering all through the month of Jaishtho (May-June). A line might be cut to incorporate kurchi and kanchan trees later. A few gawndhoraaj wouldn't be bad either. The trees that I don't like are the chhatim and kadam. Find out why shirish trees do not grow sturdy in my land.'

This letter was written in April 1940, almost exactly a year before his death. It is an extraordinary letter for two reasons: the poet's overwhelming concern for the trees of Santiniketan and his greed for more of the same. Much has also been written about Tagore's travels, his many houses in different parts of the country, his homesickness which he tried to counter by creating these new homes whenever he was on a long stay, but no such attention has been paid to his devoted upbringing of plants and trees in these new spaces. In Shillong, for instance, where he wrote his famous play *Red Oleanders*, the current owner, whose father-in-law had opened his house to Tagore, showed me the twin red oleander trees standing in the front yard. In Mungpoo too, where he stayed in Maitreyee Debi's house in the Himalayas, there was a garden full of bright mountain flowers. There still stands the remains of a pine tree that Maitreyee Debi called a favourite of the poet. 'How are the trees in Konark?' My mind goes taut and sad thinking of them,' he writes, in another letter to his daughter Mira from Penang in 1927.

When I read through these letters, experiencing the highs of a shared love, the kind lovers like me often feel while watching or reading romantic films or books, I was reminded of the many phone calls to our gardener from cities in Europe—had he changed the water in the tumbler containing the money plants, had he loosened the soil around the rose shrubs, had he taken the potted plants inside the house to the balcony to feed them some sunlight? My worries are endless—I imagine them akin to the concerns of a working woman who has put her child in day care. In such worries, we are relatives, Rabindranath and I.

I often felt terribly foolish in my desire to give my love an ancestry. Wasn't every love meant to be unique, without the baggage of history's repetition? And yet, perhaps because the nature and subject of my love was so unusual, I was curious to give this seemingly illegitimate affection a family. In Rabindranath, as also in his father and son, I found kinship. Here was a man who longed for the sight of the nagkeshor flowers when in Europe, who introduced the Vriksha-ropon Utsav, a day in the academic calendar devoted to the planting of trees. On 14 July 1928, he inaugurated the tree planting ceremony and wrote to his daughter-in-law, 'The tree planting ceremony was inaugurated by planting the bokul tree from your pot into the earth. I cannot imagine any tree more fortunate than this one. Pretty girls blew conch shells and sang while the tree was carried to the place of the yajna. Shastri mahashoy recited the Sanskrit slokas. I read out six of my poems, one after the other. The tree was welcomed and greeted with flower garlands, incense and great fanfare. Now it is doing quite well. It hasn't exhibited any sign of sadness at being transferred from your pot to the earth.'

What is most endearing about this love is Tagore's habit of baptizing his plants with new names. It was a common practice of the time to give a newly married bride a new name in her husband's family. In renaming plants with local or colloquial names, Tagore seemed to be continuing the practice. Sometimes this practice was prompted by the fact that he wasn't happy with the sound of the plant's existing name, or even its meaninglessness, at other times, it was just the joy of naming an unfamiliar flower. It was for the latter that the poet felt the deepest affection and kindness: 'Flowers bloom on stems, that is their shelter. But it is man who gives these flowers a place in his mind by naming them. There are many flowers in our country which grow without man's recognition. This indifference to flowers I have not noticed in any culture besides ours. Perhaps these flowers have names, but they are not very well known. A handful of flowers have become famous only by virtue of their fragrance—what this means is that even an indifferent person is invited into an introduction by these flowers. Our literature has permanent invitations for these flowers. I know the names of quite a few of them, and there are also those I have no acquaintance with, and nor have I tried to introduce myself to them... I am content when names of flowers match each other as end rhymes, but which race a flower belongs to is of no interest to me.'

As someone who continues to be indifferent to the names of plants and their flowers, I wondered whether it was his exposure, or perhaps the influence of the West on Tagore that had led to his desire for nomenclature for plants and trees. I felt differently from him in this case. For I had been drawn to many strangers on streets and train stations, airports and bookshops, men, women and children, but had never felt the need to ask them their names. 'What is your name?' is one of the first questions that a child is taught to answer, and I've always been uncomfortable with it. The name being the primary indicator of identity is deeply troubling to me also because we have almost no control over the names we are given and that later control our lives to an extent. Could it be only a coincidence that Shakespeare spoke about the insignificance of names in his famous 'What's in a name' line by clarifying it with the example of flowers? 'That which we call a rose would smell as sweet...'

But perhaps I was misjudging Rabindranath. Perhaps it was love that made him want to name his plants and flowers. Just as lovers give each other pet names, perhaps it was that impulse that drove him to rename his favourite trees and flowers in Uttarayan. This we learn from *Banobani*: 'I used to live in the cornermost house in Santiniketan's Uttarayan. In the courtyard of this house, my friend, the late Pearson, had planted a "bideshi", a foreign tree. After a lot of waiting, the tree began to reveal its identity through clusters of blue flowers at every node. I have always found a deep happiness in the colour blue, and every day, when I passed it, the flowers made me stand still in silence. I also wanted to speak to it as a poet, but I did not have a name with which to address it. That is why I've called the creeper "*Neelmonilata*", a blue iris creeper.'

The scientific temperament that the poet exhibits in his demand for names of unknown and unfamiliar flowers in the letter quoted earlier is contradicted by what he says about names of flowers in *Banobani*, and it is a temperament that I immediately identify with. Writing about the sweet smelling flower madhumaloti, Rabindranath says, 'This creeper must have a foreign name—I don't know it, neither do I feel the need to know it. The temples in our country have no use for these flowers, but the god who lives outside these temples finds a lot of joy and contentment in these flowers. Saraswati's verses cannot be imprisoned in temples, and that is why I have decided to worship poetry with these flowers. But I must give it a new name before that. In its beauty and essence, there is nothing foreign about it. It has not exhibited any kind of disappointment in the soil of this country, and that is why I have decided to give it a *deshi* name and make it my own.' Tagore named the flower 'Madhumanjari'.

Tagore's baptisms have the air of a colonizing mission, where the older name seems inadequate—he finds a flower that locals call 'bunophool', wild flowers or flowers of the jungle, and he decides to call the *Pavetta indica* 'bonopulok', the joy of the forest. The same year he renamed the *Ochna squarrosa*, that locals called 'ramdhoonchapa', flowers resembling a rainbow, to 'basanti', yellow. In a letter to Hemantabala Debi, he writes about the impossibility of describing the beauty of the basanti, and so he decides to send her a flower along with the letter: 'I am sending you a flower with this letter—but when it reaches you after being crushed by the postal department, it will look like a new bride that has had to endure a lot of pain from her cruel mother-in-law, and has therefore been denied its self-expression.' I found myself smiling as I read this, having sent flowers from my garden or picked up from the roadside to a distant lover or friends in foreign countries. Tagore also named the 'ghora-neem', *Millingtonia hortensis*, as 'himjhoori', a basket of dew, and reading this line from his letter, I realized, again, this identification with the tree that linked me to the poet: 'It's a very tall tree, its leaves are like those of the neem tree, the top is now covered with white flowers, it looks like my white-haired head.' Tree as man. Tree as poet.

Flowers from the forest were favourites with the Santals. The flower that they called 'langol phool', the plough-shaped flower, Rabindranath named 'agnishikha', the spires of fire. This flower first came to him as a gift from a young Santal girl, and he renamed it immediately. Pratima Debi, his daughter-in-law, recalls in her essay 'Rabindranath-er Pushpo-priti' ('Rabindranath's Love for Flowers'), the poet saying this about the backyard of the house Konark. 'This shall not be a garden of your favourite flowers. *This shall be a place for ordinary trees like me*'. I read the line again, and then again. I couldn't be sure whether my overactive imagination—that thing which, of all things, distinguished me from my plants—was superimposing my subconscious onto the poet's words. For this even casual acquaintances knew about me: that my desire was to become a tree, an ordinary tree, not a grand banyan or fig, not the colourful frangipani and jacaranda, not rose or tea shrubs. I wanted to be an ordinary tree—'ordinary' is not really a generic botanical description, I was aware, but this is what I wanted to become, grass, moss, weed, something that would not draw attention to itself, something that was of no *use* to humans, something almost nameless except as some footnote in a sincere botanist's dull diary. In Tagore, a man born to a life in the spotlight, I found an unlikely comrade and advocate for the utterly ordinary life, a near modernist urge to be an ordinary tree. One of the ways he set about to fulfil this wish was by being partial to cacti and other thorny plants. These are not a gardener's closest allies, and neither are they conventionally beautiful to the foliage-conditioned gaze. Rabindranath was around sixty years old when this 'ordinary' garden of thorny plants was set up in a corner of the backyard in Konark. Although all the cacti in this garden were not ordinary, one, for instance, that Tagore christened 'Kaata Nageshwar' after the snake god, which had even come all the way from the royal gardens in Tripura, what pleased the poet was the undemanding nature of these plants. It might have been age, who can tell, that made him want to become plants and trees with greater self-survival instincts, unlike garden plants which needed regular care and attention. Little water, little food, little attention, little care—and yet the cacti prospered. Almost in a utopian way, Rabindranath, the feted poet, the zamindar's son, longed to become one such plant.

Rathindranath, the poet's son, who is primarily responsible for the riches of the gardens of Uttarayan, is said to have studied, apart from the agricultural sciences and related botany, the Puranas, descriptions of trees by Kalidasa, Vaishnav literature, Buddhist sculpture—this rich literature of influences is to be found in Rathindranath's essay 'Bagaan' (Garden), now preserved in the archives of Rabindra Bhavan. He mentions Mughal influences, his admiration for Mughal emperors who he regarded as not only artists but scientists, and how he tried to follow their example and incorporate fountains in the Uttarayan gardens. He learnt from English, Italian and Japanese gardens. As Chattopadhyay describing the gardens says, the Uttarayan gardens are indeed a living laboratory for students of botany. *Trees of Santiniketan*, the photocopied book that I found in the bookshop, is an exhaustive catalogue of all major plant life in these gardens. I use the word 'major' with irony, of course—there never is, or never shall be, a catalogue of 'unwanted' weeds in a book such as this, just as there is no mention of beggars in the history of a country or place.

My affinity for plant life is emotional and psychological, and after trying to memorize the first few pages of the list of trees, I gave up. It was then that I realized, late though it was, that I wasn't interested so much in the trees of Santiniketan as in the people who had nurtured these trees and had perhaps wanted to become like these trees themselves. It was exactly this that was recognized by a community of sculptors and artists in 1948 when they said this of Rathindranath: 'Rathindranath Tagore knows flowers by his love for them and by science...With loving science he draws the firm logic of their patterns and gives them the space and ground on which they breathe their fragrance.'

STUDYING NATURE

The chhatim, which Rabindranath renamed shawptoporni for its seven leaves, enjoys a unique status in Santiniketan. As we have seen, the Maharshi, the poet's father, chose a small area between twin chhatim trees as his place for meditation. As I have mentioned earlier, Rabindranath was not very fond of the chhatim, and yet it was this that he chose as his equivalent of the laurel. Just as the laurel was awarded to the wise and victorious in ancient Greece, so were students at Tagore's university given a tiny branch of the chhatim on graduation day, the seven leaves, like fingers, joined at the thin wrist-like stem. Few educationists have canonized local flowers as Rabindranath had: rare is a female student who does not carry or wear a cluster of palash flowers, the flame of the forest, in her hair or as garland or bracelet on Holi, the festival of colours which is celebrated as Basanta Utsav in Santiniketan.

It is a subject introduced very early to students of Patha Bhavan, Tagore's school for children, set up in 1901. The primer is called 'Prakriti Paath' in Bangla (Nature Study: Teachers' Manual). Compiled by Anil Kumar De, it is not meant to be a textbook used in the classroom like compulsory EVS (Environment Studies) is in schools and colleges in India today. Rather, it is a book that tries to inculcate in students a love of nature. As the editor takes care to point out, Tagore's intention was not what we now call ecology. In this too, I felt a kinship. For when acquaintances who knew about my affection for plant life called me an environmentalist, I bristled. A lover does not love because she believes in the ideology of love, whatever that might be, it is because she cannot help loving. Middle-school curriculum had made me uneasy with the moral universe created by two subjects, History and Environment Science, one with its emphasis on deriving lessons from the follies of the past, the other with its future-directed fear of an apocalyptic end. Tagore's reasons for the study of life around us was pretty simple, as this letter to Kshitimohan Sen in 1909 tells us: 'We should strive to make the students familiar with the birds, animals and plant life in the ashram.' And then he catalogues the season and plant life-directed events of the ashram calendar: 'The summer-aided forest festival, the saptaparni-chhatim monsoon festival, the shefali festival in autumn, the spring festival in the sal forests...' In an essay on the education policy and ambition of the ashram in Santiniketan, Tagore laments the indifference of the conventional education system to training the five senses of children—there is so much for the ear and the eye and the hands to learn from 'nature'. And then comes the innocent confession: because the ashram school did not have funds for Physics and Chemistry laboratories, we have botany and agriculture. For this, Tagore created the annual tree-planting festival—the 'Briksha Bandana', which his translator William Radice translates as 'In Praise of Trees' instead of the more literal 'A Prayer to the Trees', which is dedicated to his botanist friend Jagadish Bose. The song begins with a belief—'O Tree, life-founder...'—and then goes on to catalogue Tagore's admiration and respect for plant life: 'O profound, silent tree', 'O friend of man', how trees 'clothe the earth with perpetual youth', and so on. One emerges from the song not merely as a convert, a new tree lover, but as someone who feels like they have lived the life of a tree from the beginning of life on this planet.

The 'nature study' module is an incredibly exciting course: students of Class Two are taught how to use their eyes, compare tall trees, use touch, their powers of smell and hearing, all of these from observing and studying the plant life in the ashram, and how the seasons affect them. The next year, in Class Three, students are taught to identify and process knowledge about colours, smell and weight through interaction with the leaves, flowers and plants of the ashram. They are also taught about time and speed and slowness through illustrations of the different kinds of plants and trees. Towards the end of the next curriculum year, in Class Four, they have learnt how to identify different kinds of soil and understand, imaginatively, which variety of plants can be expected to thrive in which kind of soil. By the time they graduate from the Fifth Standard, the students understand what constitutes 'food' for plants, humans and other animals; they also understand how to gauge and estimate time, the relationship of the plants and trees to the sun and the moon, to oxygen and carbon dioxide, and what constitutes health and illness in plants.

Rabindranath did not privilege the human over plant life, and the syllabus of this course is evidence of his refusal to treat man as more important than trees. What his students inherited through this course was a sense of trees as participant, friend and neighbour, in the ongoing drama of daily life, not merely as background. Tagore was insistent that these trees be studied as individuals, the way medical doctors and psychiatrists might study men. This pervasive equivalence of the human and plant gives a metaphysical spine to most of his poems about his favourite trees in the ashram.

⚘

What had brought me to the trees in Santiniketan was Tagore's writings on trees, particularly the tree poems. It was Rabindranath, after all, who had brought the first Bangla tree poem into my life. Rhymes learned in childhood are difficult to forget, and so the lines about the palm tree came to me as I stood close to it, the tall lanky tree shooting straight out of a mud hut. Tagore begins by calling the palm tree a single-legged creature shooting high over all other trees. It looks at the sky with longing—it wants to be a bird and fly away, Tagore tells us, thinking of its leaves as the feathers of a bird. All day the wind blows and all day the leaves move to its magnetic energy, and all day the palm tree flies with the wind, moving over the stars, as if to go to a new place. But then the wind stops blowing, and the palm tree, its upper half, the leaves that were playing a fantasy sport, return to where the rest of its body is, to the earth, to its mother. And suddenly its surroundings grow beautiful again. The tall palm, swaying in the wind, becomes a poet in Tagore's imagination. The wind stops and the palm-poet returns to the earth as it were.

The palm tree is a near autonomous person for Tagore, except for that one bit about it being chained to the earth—in this the tree is like the child in his poems, exhausted with his books and studies, asking for a break from his mother, or taking his mind on a holiday because his feet can't. This is the sense that I have in most of Tagore's tree poems, that they are trees and also people, and there is no metamorphosis but a beautiful fluidity, where one could be both, depending on desire and circumstances. His poem on the banyan tree begins with a description that makes the aged banyan tree look like an old patriarch: 'Oh you shaggy headed banyan tree'. The routine of activities that follow enhances that sense of the tree as grandfather—the child wonders how deep the tree's roots go, it desires to nestle and play in its branches like a grandchild does in a grandparent's lap.

In *The Gardener*, a long poem, a child offers flowers to an older man, who immediately likens her to the flowers she's brought: both are 'blind'.

One morning in the flower garden a blind girl came to offer me a flower chain in the cover of a lotus leaf.
I put it round my neck, and tears came to my eyes.
I kissed her and said, 'You are blind even as the flowers are.
You yourself know not how beautiful is your gift.

Had Tagore too wanted to be a tree or a flower or even a leaf? His songs paraphrase the life of flowers, fruits and trees, turn their activities into human parables, the flowers of the season become metaphors of love and waiting, the leaves move to the rhythm of his mood, the roots and veins become visible in marking relationships and history, and every now and then Tagore vents his version of back-to-nature by singing of making a journey to the forest: Jochhna raat-ey shawbai gyachhey bon-ey, Everyone's gone to the forest on this full moon night. Rabindrasangeet has become so much a part of the colloquial landscape in Bangla over the last century that this sense of plant life being a part of our emotional life is now a given—I sometimes have the sense that Bengalis care more for the trees in Tagore's songs than they do for trees on soil.

It is in the rhymes for and about children that Tagore indulges himself with the fanciful idea of being a tree most often. There is the palm and there is the banyan, yes, but there Tagore is shy about letting his desire be known, and so he hides behind metaphors. In a poem like the one about the champa tree, he doesn't hold himself back any longer:

> Supposing I became a champa flower, just for fun, and grew on a branch high up that tree, and shook in the wind with laughter and danced upon the newly budded leaves, would you know me, mother?
> You would call, 'Baby, where are you?' and I should laugh to myself and keep quite quiet.
> I should slyly open my petals and watch you at your work.
> When after your bath, with wet hair spread on your shoulders, you walked through the shadow of the champa tree to the little court where you say your prayers, you would notice the scent of the flower, but not know that it came from me.
> When after the midday meal you sat at the window reading Ramayana, and the tree's shadow fell over your hair and your lap, I should fling my wee little shadow on to the page of your book, just where you were reading.
> But would you guess that it was the tiny shadow of your little child?
> When in the evening you went to the cowshed with the lighted lamp in your hand, I should suddenly drop on to the earth again and be your own baby once more, and beg you to tell me a story.
> 'Where have you been, you naughty child?'
> 'I won't tell you, mother.' That's what you and I would say then.

This is Tagore's version of metamorphosis then—an interspecies fluidity, where one could move between human and tree bodies. It is interesting that in all these poems, Tagore chooses the day life of a tree

Sumana Roy

and the night life of a human. Apart from the oxygen-carbon dioxide sharing that distinguishes day labour from the tree's night shift, Tagore might be pointing to something else: night might be a more luxuriant time for the artist and the child, as the day is for a food-cooking plant. Humans don't like cooking in the middle of the night after all. This is not my speculation alone, for Tagore tells us this in *Chhelebyala*, a memoir of his childhood: 'I've always been a night loving boy... The shadow of trees on the terrace on a full moon night is like an alpana of dreams.' This is the same terrace that his sister-in-law turned into a 'garden' full of chameli, jasmine, rajnigandha, oleander and dolonchaapa trees. And it is in the same memoir that Tagore confesses to a boyhood experiment with 'flower ink'. The gardener in Shilaidaha, where he spent his early adult life, would arrange the day's flowers in a vase every day. The variety of colours in the vase stoked Tagore's desire to write in that colourful language—it wasn't too *unnatural* a thought for a young poet to want to write like flowers after all. So the flowers were crushed and passed through several sieves and tools, but there was no ink that could be filled into the belly of a fountain pen.

Among all of Tagore's work on this person-as-plant fantasy, my favourite is the short story called 'Bawlai'. The narrator begins by giving us examples of people who exhibit characteristics that are not human—some take after animals, some show similarities with music. Bawlai, the narrator's nephew, behaved like a tree. As a child, he would stand and stare silently, like trees do, showing no curiosity for new places that boys of his age did. When it rained, he behaved like a happy tree in July, when it grew very hot, he moved about bare-chested, embracing the heat like trees do. He was always tree-like: in the month of Magh, he behaved like the mango tree beginning to bloom; in Phalgun, he became a flowering sal tree. A quiet child who did not indulge in much human conversation, he thought the grass in the mountains a playful living mass which kept on rolling down. It wasn't a fixed thing, and soon, rolling down the grassy fields of the Himalayas, he began to resemble grass. The deodar forests would fill him with awe, and he would be curious about their history, just as young saplings would fill him with worry about the future—'Then? What next?'

Bawlai hurt when someone plucked a flower off a plant or when boys threw stones at the gooseberry tree for its fruit, but he was saddest when the grass cutter came—not only would he cut the grass and cause it pain, the man would also weed away all the 'ordinary' plants and saplings that Bawlai loved. Only Bawlai knew about the secret life of seeds that had fallen from trees overhead and had now struck a tiny root in the ground.

A motherless child, Bawlai lived with his uncle and aunt. And so he would plead with his aunt, 'Please ask him not to cut my plants'. To which his aunt would grow impatient and reply, 'Don't be mad. Don't you see how the grass is growing into a jungle?' How old was Bawlai? Though he was only a little child, he was as old as the earth's forests—he carried their spirit in him. Everyone made jokes about him because of this.

One day, as his uncle was reading the newspaper, little Bawlai came to show him a tiny sapling. What tree would this grow into? It was the sapling of a silk cotton tree that had just taken root, and Bawlai had been wrong in showing it to his uncle. I'll ask the gardener to uproot it, it grows very quickly, said the uncle. Little Bawlai then sought his aunt's intervention—let his plant be, she told her husband.

It grew at a fierce pace, almost bolstered by Bawlai's affection, and it grew into a nagging eyesore in his uncle's eyes. For it stood right in the middle of the pathway. His uncle bargained with him—he'd get another silk cotton tree planted near the boundary wall, but this one must go. Young Bawlai wouldn't have that. And so the tree continued to grow. In the meantime, Bawlai's father arrived to take him away to Shimla, where he'd get an education before he was sent to England for higher studies. The childless couple, who had raised him for ten years, was heartbroken but they had to let him go.

A few years later, Bawlai wrote a letter to his aunt asking for a photograph of his silk-cotton tree. He was to have visited them before his trip to England but that hadn't been possible. And so his aunt asked her husband to ask for a photographer to visit them at home. But Bawlai's uncle, unable to tolerate it anymore, had got the silk cotton tree cut only a few days ago. She was shocked—she refused to eat and

Sumana Roy

speak to him for days.

The story ends with this simple but resonant thought: the tree had been her Bawlai's reflection after all, his double.

Now I often look at people, both family and strangers, and wonder which tree could be their double.

Part V

I Want to Do with You What Spring Does with the Cherry Trees
—Pablo Neruda, *'Love Poem XIV'*

HAVING SEX WITH A TREE

Would I miss my sex life if I turned into a tree?

'I want a boyfriend like a banyan tree.' This is the opening line of Sharanya Manivannan's prose poem, 'Boyfriend like a Banyan Tree'. Why a banyan of all trees? 'A man who's a forest unto himself, with conspiracies of birds, and secret blossoms, and shaded places; a matrix generous enough for the world. And into this forest I will wander, a beloved of the world, and walk beneath the aegis of his boughs knowing that the same love that roots them raises me. I will become entangled.' Lovers are known to turn each other into versions of themselves— rubbing oneself with earth like a tree, becoming 'entangled' like the roots of a banyan, speaking in silences to a lover like we imagine trees doing. This is a woman who has been left exhausted by human lovers.

I was reading these lines in early March. There was the intimacy of the weather, spring being the carrier and courier of secrets. What secrets might I want to keep from my tree-lover?

How exactly does it feel to marry a tree? The poet Nitoo Das writes about the memory of getting married to a plantain plant at the age of eleven, that last detail giving the poem its title:

> I swore never to starve again
> and never marry
> a plantain plant again.
> We never met after we wedded
> or I'd have feasted on all his parts:
> flowers, fruits, shoots.

The little girl's frustration at being married to an unspeaking plantain as part of an Assamese puberty ritual, the entire atmosphere standing in but also surviving on a mimicry of sex, with the adult rituals of marriage being replicated in tiny but detailed measures, takes all the romance out of this tree-woman relationship. But, then, which teenager would list a tree as its ideal companion?

Between the banyan lover and the angry young plantain-wife is the orphan girl Uma in Aparna Sen's 1989 film *Sati*. Tortured by an aunt with whom she is forced to live after the death of her parents, Uma is mute. It is early nineteenth-century Bengal, and an astrologer has predicted a life of widowhood for her. The elders in the village decide that getting her married to a tree is the only way to save her—the tree would die and take with it the curse of widowhood. Uma, lonely and unloved, finds companionship in the unspoken love of the banyan tree to which she is eventually married off. But Uma is soon found to be pregnant and even the superstitious villagers are not convinced that the father of the child in the girl's womb could be the banyan. The truth is that Uma was raped by a local schoolteacher one stormy night, but how is a mute girl to tell that to the world? The film ends quite melodramatically, with the villagers discovering two dead bodies after a stormy night. The banyan, struck by fierce lightning, now lies dead, and lying against it is its wife Uma, her forehead smeared with blood where the married woman's vermilion is usually applied. And so Uma becomes a sati, sacrificing her life upon the death of her husband. It was the companionship of silence shared by Uma and the tree that had appealed most to me in Aparna Sen's adaptation of Kamal Majumdar's story when I first watched the film as a teenager. I also speculated about the parentage of the child in Uma's womb—was it really not possible for a tree to grow inside a woman's womb? (Why did our mothers warn us about swallowing orange pips then?) And with it the allied question: why was I thinking of the banyan as Uma's husband all the while? Why wasn't I thinking of tree-woman love as same sex love?

One of my favourite stories of such a romance is by the young writer Adrienne Lang. I discovered her quite by chance from a Facebook post by the writer Amitava Kumar. Lang was Kumar's student at Vassar College, and I was so taken by her illustrated story called, quite simply,

'The Tree' that I requested the professor for a formal introduction. I later looked for Lang on Facebook where the world now does its data mining. I was immediately hooked to her profile photo: the twenty-two-year-old had two giant vegetable soft toys in her arms, a carrot and broccoli. I had the feeling of having encountered a stranger I had no option but to like very much. Lang's story that had first got me interested me in her held in it some of my natural insecurities as a lover. A woman comes home to find that her boyfriend has turned into a tree. This was just as well. She was tired of always worrying about where he went when he wasn't with her, and what he did, and who he talked to at work, and what he looked at on his computer, and who he emailed, and what he bought, and what he was thinking about all of the times that she had asked 'What are you thinking about?' and he had said, 'Oh, nothing.' The boyfriend turned into a fig tree. She ate the figs with her cereal, thinking of this as his way of 'apologizing' to her, as a tree, for all of the things she suspected he had done as a man.

Eating a partner without causing them violence must be the best form of erotica, but Lang introduces a sly line in this seemingly simple story. The woman is insecure, she is exhausted from playing patrol police on her boyfriend all the time, she worries about his loyalty, she is even convinced, perhaps without evidence, that the man has done things he shouldn't have. And so this is his apology—his turning into a tree.

Are our sins sublimated once we become trees? And isn't it strange that naturally adulterous beings like trees could become tropes for conventional romantic loyalty? Are trees, then, our best selves?

There is the real life story of Emma McCabe who wants to marry a tree she loves—she calls the tree 'Tim' and has sex with him. In an interview with the UK's *Closer* magazine, McCabe said, 'My feelings are genuine. I've had boyfriends, but never connected with anyone like Tim. I'm in love and would like to get married.' She added: 'He fulfils my emotional and sexual needs. I orgasm by rubbing against the bark naked. I love the feeling of skin-on-bark contact, which gives me a more pleasurable pain sensation, and the feel of his leaves against my skin makes me tingle. I have sex with him every week—it's the best I've ever had!' And it's a monogamous relationship: 'I look at other trees, but don't touch—I wouldn't cheat on Tim. I'd like to get married, but it would be a low-key ceremony with family.'

There are many who have married trees. In November 2013, the Peruvian actor Richard Torres married a tree in Buenos Aires—he wanted to highlight environmental problems around the survival of trees, but ended up in a long kiss with the tree he had chosen as his bride. Men from Orissa who have been widowed twice are often married to a tree in the belief that it will 'absorb' the bad luck. And young girls from Nepal continue to be married to wood apple trees. M. S. Randhawa, in his book *The Cult of Trees and Tree-Worship in Buddhist-Hindu Sculpture*, mentions a man resting under an udumbara tree and looking at it sadly while thinking of his childless marriage. 'If only my wife was like this tree, what happiness we would have,' he thinks, and then, chancing upon a 'hole' in the tree at a height almost the man's waist, he 'goes' into it. 'In due time a human child was born from one of the figs and he was the father of the Dumariya clan.'

Sumana Roy

LOVING TREES

Imagine the tree naked. Imagine grass as lover. How would you embrace your lover then? Imagine moss as an ex. What a misalliance. To love a tree is to be a permanently exiled lover.

I should know.

At first there is curiosity, and strangers read that as a sign of plant affection, a borderline love of the kind that allows them to forgive children their attachment to favourite toys for instance. But when the same group of people begin to see you travelling with the same plant every day, the first pinch of shock arrives. From plant lover I become—Bengalis are more direct in their vocabulary for such people, calling them 'mental', adjective as noun—a patient in need of counselling. This wouldn't happen if I was travelling with a pet animal or a human partner or companion, so unused are we to the sight of plant life travelling in public transport. It was to challenge this perhaps that the Chicago subway train was transformed into a garden on wheels as part of the Art on Track Festival in 2011. A slideshow of photographs of the event on the Inhabitat website shows surprised smiles on the faces of commuters, an indulgence allowed to the grass-covered seats where they would be seated on any other day, potted plants by the window and other such spaces, the men and women standing in the corridor, still recovering from the surprise. But imagine if this were to happen every day—would the commuters not protest? It is one thing to not get a seat because a fellow human passenger happens to be sitting on it and quite another to have a seat given to ticketless grass.

A taxi driver from Calcutta solved this problem by turning the overhead carrier of his cab into a grass bed and filling the rear board with short potted plants. The man's name is Bapi and he is now recognized by the name 'Bapi Green Taxi'. He does not charge his passengers an extra amount—the only leverage he allows himself is a request to every passenger to return home and plant a tree. There is, without a doubt, a moral ecological propellant in this initiative, but what I take from this story is a tale about love, a man who cannot tolerate biraha, separation from his lover, someone who has loved so much and so passionately that he is filled with surplus. This is why he implores those who have not loved or not known love like he has—go home, take a lover, let your lover change you and the world, go, plant a tree.

⚶

My conditioning in romantic love had given me a long list of criteria I expected any lover of mine to satisfy.

However, these would need to be recalibrated when it came to trees. Any notions of space and self-reliance that seemed to mark successful modern relationships were completely useless in the tree-human romantic relationship. So was reciprocity, the need that soured so many human relationships. How was one to think of reciprocity in a creature that neither spoke nor was influenced by human languages? The Bengali film-maker Srijeet Mukherjee, for instance, tried to solve this problem by giving the tree in his film *Nirbaak* human characteristics: sap becomes semen in an act of onanism by the tree, this propelled by the sight of a woman resting in its shade.

That is passion, but there's also romance.

And the epistolary quotient of love relationships? I've loved writing letters to my lover—they contained the most secretive part of me, one that I was ashamed to otherwise see manifest. In letters I was able to love unconscious of any gaze. This was also true of secret meetings, hide-and-seek, keeping and missing appointments. There are spaces that indulge this. But how was one to meet a tree who would not move out of its home? I compared it cruelly with relationships with the differently-abled and regretted it immediately. But curiosity was natural—I had seen the fixity of location affecting relationships between people. How could it not for plants? There was the other matter about privacy. Romantic love demands a tent if not a house. Imagine a tree inside a tent. End of Love Story. There is also the knock on the door, literal and metaphorical, that initiates or causes a temporary pause to the lovers' actions and conversations. How can one visit a tree without needing to knock on the door? This uncertainty, the ambiguity between being welcome and being rebuffed, will always mark the life of a tree-human relationship. There is the chorus of I-want-my-space all around me—how am I to know whether I'm being intrusive?

Possessiveness was the other worry. I have been a possessive lover. Plant life, by its very biological nature, does not understand monogamy. Loyalty is an alien concept, adultery an everyday thing. How would I adjust to this new world after years—centuries?—of social conditioning? There were also different kinds of love—a farmer's love is not the same as a tourist's. The farmer's is also a gatekeeper's life, sometimes like a spouse's. In my relationship with strange and familiar trees, I was both. I now realize that this allowed me to love them like a tree, loving one and the many, the gardener and the admiring passer-by. Waking up beside a lover must count as one of the most rewarding experiences of being in a relationship. The person still asleep might receive an unexpected—unexpected because sleep is free of expectations—kiss on the eyelids, the closed eyes. How was one to inaugurate such a day with a tree? Films had invented a rather cute stand-in for this—kissing flower buds that open into flowers. But a kiss demands reciprocity. There is nothing more cruel than a one-sided kiss. You look for the 'face' of the tree, hoping it will turn towards you like a human lover. But it has no 'face'. Since love is based on exchange, you might wait for the tree's saliva, some evidence that would ratify the pantomime of lust. Here there is none.

The other kind of reciprocity has to do with the exchange of gifts between lovers—the conventional flowers and chocolates, books and soft toys. What is one to gift a tree? Certainly not soft toys or flowers or trees, for there are none, only educational toys like clay and plastic fruits in a nursery classroom. The use of real flowers to express love would be a thing of irony—plucking flowers off a tree and presenting them to it might be a bit like chopping off a woman's fingers and then gift-wrapping them as an anniversary gift. The opposite option, of plucking flowers off a neighbouring tree of a different species and presenting them to the lover-tree, could be analogical to sending a strange woman's hair stored inside a pendant to a lover? How would you prove your innocence—loyalty—then? Lovers are known to swear on each other as a mark of their honesty to each other, they sometimes swear on god, on the sun and the moon, on mothers and their ambition and success, but who has ever heard a lover swear on a tree or flower or fruit?

I once asked a male friend whether he'd like to have a tree as a mate. He replied with a joke, using the laboured example of a wife's nagging. Trees have no memory, not of pain, neither of pleasure. It is this that makes them tabula rasas—they are lovers like no other. History here was unchangeably one-sided—the lover remembers the tree, the tree doesn't remember her at all. Conditioned as we are to memory—of birthdays, good days, bad days—being a great seismograph in relationships, it would be both exciting and frustrating to return to a new lover every evening, an old lover with whom one must begin anew with every meeting. And I suddenly found myself becoming completely accepting of this, I who never forget to remind my husband about his forgetfulness about birthdays and anniversaries.

Kahlil Gibran's advisory lines from 'On Marriage' ends with an illustration of a good marriage from the plant world: 'And the oak tree and the cypress grow not in each other's shadow.' The natural process in which trees 'marry' each other is called 'inosculation'—called 'husband' and 'wife' trees, the two trees grow adjacent to each other until their branches conjoin. I've seen trees being married to each other in full-bodied Hindu ceremonies, with grand feasts and wedding guests representing the groom and the bride. A piece of red cloth, often considered to be sacred to Hindus, is used to wrap the trunks of the two trees in an embrace. I discovered several such married trees on National Highway 31 on my way to work—in my inescapably anthropomorphized mind, it seemed like a cinematic freeze of the most romantic kind, two lovers in an eternal embrace, but when months passed and the embrace grew tighter as new branches grew into each other, I began to hear that modern phrase every time I saw them: 'I need some space'. Ellison Banks Findly gives examples from the *Vrikshayurveda* where a 'Shyama creeper nearing the blossoming of flowers, closely clinging to a tree looks like a damsel' and Kalidasa's *Abhigyan Shakuntalam* where Shakuntala chances upon the married couple of jasmine vines and a mango tree.

In a Naga folk tale, a young princess grows up as a friend to a peepul tree until she falls in love with it. When her father organizes a swayamvar for her to choose a husband from princes from neighbouring kingdoms, she refuses. She has set her eyes on a young man who does not wear the royal robes. The princess's maid follows the man who hurriedly disappears into the jungle. The next day the princess discovers the truth about the man and the tree: he was a Naga prince who had been trapped by an evil magician inside the peepul tree. Versions of this tale—of a beautiful woman falling in love with a tree only to discover a human lover trapped inside it—exist in almost all cultures.

At the other end of the spectrum is the folk tale about women turning into trees. The most well-known of these is the one the poet A. K. Ramanujan collected and translated as 'A Flowering Tree'. An old woman has two daughters in a kingdom where the king has a daughter and a son of marriageable age. The old woman is poor and works hard for a living. And so the youngest daughter, eager to help supplement the family income, tells her sister about the rituals of turning into a tree. There is scepticism at first but it soon turns out to be a real thing: the younger sister turns into a tree, the older one plucks her beautiful flowers, pours water on her from a pitcher and the girl is restored to her human form again. This, of course, takes place without their mother's knowledge. They make lovely garlands out of these flowers and sell them to the queen. The prince, who is completely taken by the unearthly beauty of these flowers, follows the flower-selling girls to their house and spies on the process of transformation. He then manages to convince his father to arrange his marriage with the girl.

A few days into the marriage, the prince wants his wife to turn into a tree so that they can sleep together on the flowers. She refuses, then pleads, but he won't see reason. And so begins this nightly ritual. The flowering girl's sister-in-law, who has spied on them, tricks the tree-woman into accompanying her group of friends on an outing. Once there, she is compelled by them to turn into a tree. She warns them not to hurt her or cause her branches and flowers any harm, but the sister-in-law and her friends are so delighted at this game that they plunder her body and leave without restoring her to her human self. The tree-woman becomes a 'thing' and is washed ashore into a different kingdom where she fortunately finds care. After a series of events, her husband, living a hermit's life, searching for her everywhere, is now united with the 'thing' and finally, after the bandaging of bruised and wounded leaves and branches, the tree becomes a woman again.

Ramanujan, explaining the tale through a gendered lens, writes, 'It becomes almost a sexual ritual, a display of her spectacular talent to turn him on, so that they can sleep together on the flowers from her body...when she is returned to her human state, she too is left ravaged, mutilated. It is a progressive series of violations till she finally ends up being a "thing"...When is a woman safe in such a society? She is most vulnerable when she is a tree. She can neither speak nor move. She is most open to injury when she is most attractive, when she is exercising her gift of flowering... She can be made whole only by becoming the tree again, becoming vulnerable again, and trusting her husband to graft and heal her broken branches.'

Pain is a typo in all emotional relationships. How can it not be there in tree-human love? And so the tautology of pain every time the woman is forced to change into a tree against her will. I also wondered whether the outcome of the tale might have been different had the tree in the story been a man and this been a story of homosexual love. I say this because I had found that loving trees, they without visible sex differentiation, had rendered their gender completely irrelevant to my consciousness. Their lack of visible sex, I have to confess, had made

Sumana Roy

me more comfortable with them than I had ever been with humans.

࿐

The imagined reactions of families to such a relationship bothered me. Honour killings were so common in this country—families killed lovers who had married against the wishes of their families. Would they kill a woman who had left home for a tree? Would my family be ashamed if I took a tree as a lover? No matter how moral and utilitarian the nature of the tree-human relationship, a romance between the two would be considered outrageous. I thought this terribly lopsided. A friend naughtily pointed me to her great reservoir of knowledge about erotica and pornography with carrots and radishes as sex toys, but that was that. There are no relationships in pornographic settings—climax is the only target.

Inequality seemed to be necessary to keep marriages happy, or at least, stable. A marriage, I had discovered, wasn't a democracy. From a zoocentric perspective, plants lacked brains. From another perspective, they were more self-sufficient than all animals. How might that inequality play out in a tree-human marriage? At such moments of reflection, my niece's words came to me sometimes, she who'd asked me with a child's innocence how I, who found intelligence the magnetic centre in people, could want to marry a tree. There was another lack that I kept silent about: I loved people who made me laugh. But the trees I knew had exhibited no sense of humour yet.

࿐

I thought of invitations to parties and social events and how it might look to walk in with a potted plant ferried on wheels and then dance with it through the evening. When a friend invited me for a New Year's party, I smiled at the inconsequentiality of a new calendar year for my plants. I also realized that these were outrageous thoughts, but of all my identities, this was most precious to me—that I was a lover.

My mind grazed on such thoughts all the time. If I married a tree, would I need to change my surname? Sumana Tree? Or would the tree take on my surname—Tree Roy? Or would I choose a part for

How I Became a Tree   117

the whole—Sumana Flower, Sumana Trunk, Sumana Leaf? I laughed. It showed up the surname-changing business associated with the marriages of people for what it really was—an exercise in hilarity. Some of these thoughts took root in my dreams. In one such dream, I ordered a table for two when I took my periwinkle lover with me to a restaurant.

When I returned from such dreams, an old question returned to haunt me. Why had the sight of trees never aroused me sexually?

Part VI

One Tree is Equal to Ten Sons
—*Matsya Purana*

PLANTS AS CHILDREN

Friends and strangers, in varying measures, tried to impress upon me the need to have—and love—a child of my own blood. I was, of course, weary of explaining. Why was it not evident to these otherwise well-meaning people that the most important relationship in my life was with a man who was not related to me by blood? I wrote answers to these questions in my mind, but like an examinee who fails a memory test at the most crucial moment, I lapsed into silence when the attacks came. I wrote poems, some of which brought me prefaces to happiness—some kind readers of these poems called them my 'children'. I did not object. Apart from stool, urine, vomit and snot, humans are happy to claim every other production as offspring—ideas, poems, music, literature, paintings. Was it the capitalist temperament of our times that prevented people from seeing trees as children, since they are incapable of serving as pension schemes for their parents? It was blood, human blood, that would nurse me in my old age; nothing else could, I was told.

While I read poems and stories about the many green children produced by human parents, I also grew adamant in my belief that the parenting I had chosen was in no way inferior to the production of human children, those that might have carried my blood. Living things, as the category goes, were biological photocopying machines—they could only produce a likeness of themselves. Hence the surprise—and consequent punishment—when queens in folk tales produced animals from their wombs. The more I reflected on it, the deeper my suspicion grew: we were so scared of the Other that we refused to give it space even in our imaginary wombs. The only legitimate biological relationship that we were allowed to have with those who did not look like us was through our mouths: we bite, chew, mash, gnash and swallow all kinds of plants and animals, everything except humans that is. It was this, I began to realize, that had given birth to my unease with vegetarianism, this unquestioning and amoral consumption of plant life that privileged animal life over plants. We do not—cannot—eat our human children because that would be a gruesome act of cannibalism. But my plants? My tiny kitchen garden with its enthusiastic sprouting of herbs was specifically meant for indulging the tongue. And yet I felt no deep suffering to see them thus bullied and tortured by the cook. For this I had no answer.

☙

At work, quite by accident, I discovered the existence of something called 'Child Care Leave'. I was aware that no legislation in the next two centuries would make a woman like me, who thought of birthing as more than a biological process, be eligible for 'Maternity Leave'. That kind of privilege was for relationships forged by blood, not for bloodless nonhumans. But surely Child Care Leave could be made available to me? I waited for the right words to phrase my application letter.

Through all this, the metaphor of blood never left me, not as the children I was asked to produce, and more significantly perhaps not inside me. My haemoglobin count, doctors reminded me from time to time, was abysmally low. Once, when I saw a young son telling his mother that he had had a litre of blood extracted out of him, this to be put inside her to help her recuperate after her surgery, I was filled with wonder at the thought of a child giving his mother blood as she had once given him during his tenancy in her womb. But my fancy stretched further. Was such reciprocity ever possible in the monologous relationship I shared with my plants? I had given them care, attention, affection, water, everything except sunlight, which I was, of course, incapable of producing. Could they not give me blood when I needed it most?

One day our gardener, always planning his next strategy, one that would help him get an advance, got me a bunch of thorny leaves. The ill are so needy for attention that they are prone to trust anyone, even those with a history of lies. I mistook the bunch of greens for a rustic bouquet. He had understood my indifference to the glamour of flowers at last, I allowed myself the thought. In that happiness was also the sweetness of victory, of having been able to convert a gardener to grow plants that did not necessarily produce colour for the eye. But all these thoughts found only a moment's rest, for Ajay-da, with his difficulties in speech, turned towards me and said, 'Eat this blood.'

The details needed excavation: the leaves of this thorny plant were to be boiled in water and its consistency reduced to a thick syrup. A few spoons of this every day and I would be cured. I would discover its English and scientific names much later, when I would find the energy to sit up before the computer. Until then the Bangla name sufficed: kuleykhara. This green concoction would cure me of anaemia—I began to think of every green sip as blood transfusion from a bottle into my veins.

Green to red, chlorophyll to blood.

Colours must ripen. Or they leave no progeny.

THE CURIOUS BOTANIST

The first words that came to my ears as I climbed up the stairs to Mayapuri, the botanist Jagadish Chandra Bose's house in Darjeeling, were about his childlessness. Mr Rai, the caretaker, a Nepali man in his mid-sixties was explaining 'Life' Science to the woman who had accompanied me. Her name was Arti, and ten years ago, when I had taught in a college in this small Himalayan town, she used to help me with the housekeeping. Like me, she had no biological children. Arti turned to look back at me. Perhaps she wanted to protect me from the sound of his words.

'It is because he was childless that he began thinking of these trees and plants as his children,' the man repeated.

It was true that I had once indulged the same thought. In his essays in Bangla, I had often paused to note that when Bose wrote about plants, generic or specific, he referred to them as infants, and sometimes a slightly older child. I was, of course, carrying personal baggage: having been married for well over a decade but having not produced children as a 'fruit' of that relationship, I was aware of the metaphorical and psychological narrative that attended this analogy between children and fruition, especially when it came to clarifying the obsessive affection for plant life to be found in some of those who had no human children.

As I climbed up the stairs, staring at the neatly maintained garden of exquisite mountain flowers to my left, I felt a kinship with Bose that was not new. It was to discover more about that ancestry of plantlovingness that I had made this journey to Darjeeling, to his house which he had, quite fancifully, called 'Mayapuri', 'a fantasy land'. Part of the property was new, having been built from the state exchequer as a kind of outpost to the Bose Institute, one of India's premier scientific research institutions that Bose had founded in 1917.

I peeped in through the glass windows, and when Arti joked whether I was hoping to sight Bose's ghost inside, I became self-conscious. I was embarrassed to tell her that I was wondering whether—even hoping that—I would find a potted plant from Bose's time inside, a kind of living relic as it were. For the next half hour, Mr Rai showed us Bose's bedroom and study, his typewriter, his mirrors and his hat stand, his leather batik bag, photos of Bose's parents resting against a wooden wall, the fireplace where I imagined Bose burnt those he loved (logs of wood), the props of a life lived according to one's wishes. But before all these were revealed to me, I stood in front of a carved wooden door, its intricate designs reminiscent of old temples of India from the fifteenth and sixteenth centuries, and wondered—did Bose ever think of the pain wood-carving might have caused these dead trees, the chisel on the wood?

But had I? Wasn't wood my favourite material for furniture?

I was coming to Bose's mountain house from Roy Villa on Lebong Cart Road. This was the house where Sister Nivedita—a writer and social worker of Scots-Irish descent whose original name had been Margaret Elizabeth Noble—a close friend of Jagadish and his wife Abala, had first hosted them in Darjeeling. I cannot explain why I had gone to Roy Villa—the house had borne the brunt of Darjeeling's violent post-colonial history. There was almost nothing to mark the life of Nivedita and her illustrious guests in it anymore—taken over by armed volunteers of the Gorkhaland movement, it had been converted into a base and dormitory for amateur 'soldiers'. The West Bengal Chief Minister, Mamata Banerjee, a devotee of Swami Vivekananda, who had shared close ties with Sister Nivedita, had struck a bargain with the Gorkha Janmukti Morcha, the political outfit leading the movement for autonomy—the West Bengal government would hand over Roy Villa to the Ramakrishna Mission Nivedita Educational and Cultural Centre; a 'total development programme for poor children' now operates from there. And yet, despite such foreknowledge I had gone there, I cannot say why. In spite of the town's expansion and the accompanying deforestation, the house continued to look and feel deserted. It was at the furthest end of town—the dense growth of trees added to the eeriness. There is an onomatopoeic word in Bangla that best explains the atmosphere of uncanny stillness there: 'thawmthawmay'. I'd stood alone on the pathway leading to the house, looking at the trees, trying to guess their age, I wondered how many of them Bose might have seen a hundred years ago. Our historical markers bother me—there are records of visitors to historical places but absolutely none that give us a history of trees.

Fortunately there was no cell phone connectivity there. I wouldn't have known that at all had two neighbouring sounds not entered my ears with this complaint. After the two adult voices, one male, the other female, there was a child's cry. The adult voices began complaining again. My Nepali is rusty now, after nearly a decade of non-use, but I could guess the subject: the couple was complaining about how child unfriendly this place was. A third voice suddenly entered the conversation, an elderly male it seemed to me, who explained it thus: 'Sister Nivedita did not have children. Vivekananda didn't either. Neither did Jagadish Bose and his wife. How could such a place be child friendly?' Laughter followed, and I found myself slowly driven out by it.

At Mayapuri, which was at the other end of town, investigating the adjacent garden for unfamiliar flowers, I was reminded of Bose placing value on the garden as metaphor: this institute was now a mountainside campus of the Bose Institute he established in Calcutta, and that he had called the 'Study and Garden of Life', where 'the Laboratory merges imperceptibly into the gardens, which is the true laboratory for the study of Life.'

Writing to his friend Rabindranath Tagore on 20 May 1899, Bose described his place of stay in Darjeeling: 'I have been leading the most passive life here. Where I live there is not a single sound of the human (it's beyond Birch Hill); only bird cries and the Himalayas in front of my eyes. If you could come, it would be good. Can you not come for a few days?' The unmistakable solitude, described here, of the surroundings in this already quiet sanatorium town of the last years of the nineteenth century was, without a doubt, responsible for Bose's contemplation on the invisible and silent life of plants. Thoreau, Nietzsche, Kant, Kierkegaard, Descartes, Pascal, Spinoza, Augustine, even the Buddha, all those who had been able to change the trajectory of human thought with their philosophies and insights had been the outcome of long hours of solitude, of a life spent away from human inhabited spaces, almost solely in the company of trees. Far from the madding crowd had now become a touristy expression, but there was something to be had—gained and lost—from an engagement with solitude. I felt stifled by city life. On the margins of the town in which I worked were gigantic buildings whose skeletons (what else could I call these works in progress?) looked intimidating and invincible—I complained endlessly to my co-passengers about the height of these buildings, and how claustrophobic they made me feel. And yet, when I taught in a classroom on the second floor of the college building, I was always glad and relieved to notice the tall tree whose branches eavesdropped outside the window. Many of these aged trees were taller than the building but they generated no annoyance or suffocation in me. Similarly, when I complained about the overpopulated spaces we were forced to live in, I was struck by how illogical it was in a way. Classrooms, staff rooms, offices, theatres, shopping malls, markets, buses, trains, and their stations—all of these, with their shifting numbers, made me want to flee human contact. To escape, I wanted to go to a forest, for instance. It did not strike me then that I wanted to leave one overpopulated place for another—only the unit had changed from humans to trees.

I wanted to believe that Jagadish Bose had felt the same way, for the quiet solitude of a life in pre-touristy Darjeeling a hundred years ago must have been a life lived mostly among plant life. I had not been able to locate Assyline Villa, where Bose had lived with his wife in Darjeeling. The name of the house had come to me in a letter the scientist had written to Rabindranath Tagore, thanking him for the gift of a plant 'cutting' that the poet had sent from the plains of Bengal. I remembered the date on the letter distinctly: 16 May 1905. By some miraculous coincidence, I had come looking for Bose's mountain houses exactly on that day, a hundred and eight years later.

⚘

One of the things that Bose had in common with his plants was an indifference to money. He had invented the wireless two years before Guglielmo Marconi did, but Bose's lack of interest in money, and his belief in science as something that was to be shared without any thought for personal profit, had prevented him from applying for a patent. In a letter to Rabindranath Tagore, he mentions an encounter with an English gentleman in London after Bose had refused to 'sell' his invention: 'There is money in it—let me take out a patent for you. You do not know what money you are throwing away... I will only take half a share in the profit—I will finance it...' Bose refused. The 'notes' that he had left on the table for the demonstration disappeared. That they appeared in a tweaked guise a couple of years later, with Marconi's name on it, is now common knowledge. This refusal to forge an alliance between scientific inventions and commerce marked his inaugural address at the Bose Institute in 1917 when he said, 'The discoveries made will thus become public property. No patents will ever be taken.'

Jagadish Bose had the curiosity of a detective, but unlike the Intelligence Bureau or Scotland Yard, he was not interested in the secret lives of people but of plants. Just as detectives use CCTV cameras and other spyware, Bose created his own instruments to spy on the secret life of plants—the Resonant Recorder could calibrate the level of excitement generated by external stimulus; the electric probe could identify parts of the plant which behaved like neurons in humans; the Phytograph recorded the heartbeat-like rhythms of the Desmodium plant; the Plant Potograph measured the rate at which plants drank water; there was an Automatic Potograph; the Bubler Instrument recorded a plant's relationship with water; the Plant Sphygmograph measured the expansion and contraction in cells as a result of their drinking water; the famous Crescograph, for which Bose was praised and ridiculed in equal measure, recorded a plant's rate of growth in its own 'script' as it were; a more sophisticated version of this was the Magnetic Crescograph which produced more accurate records of the plant's growth; and there was the Photosynthetic Recorder which kept track of the plant's relationship with light and oxygen. These are all extremely complex instruments, and as I read about them and saw illustrated diagrams of their innards, I began to wonder whether Jagadish Bose had actually been a botanist interested in the physiology of plants. Wasn't he trying to be a plant psychologist? I identified with that outrageous desire, and hence my elective affinity..

Bose recognized the interstitial nature of his investigation himself—'I was unconsciously led into the border region of physics and physiology and was amazed to find boundary lines vanishing and points of contact emerge between the realm of the Living and Non-Living...A universal reaction seemed to bring together metal, plant and animal under a common law. They all exhibited essentially the same phenomena of fatigue and depression together with possibilities of recovery and of exaltation, yet also that of permanent irresponsiveness which is also associated with death.' The reactions his work elicited among scientists bound by their disciplinary regimen made Bose speak out time and again about the 'caste system' in the sciences. One was to follow the rituals of one's caste-discipline—inter-disciplinarity was still a long time away. Again, because frustration and rejection bind people more than joy, I was repeatedly reminded of people, especially botanists, wondering why I was always curious about the life of plants when I did not know how to read the behaviour of their cells under an electron microscope.

About something Bose remained certain—that his mission was to bring the 'secret' of plant life to us. For a long time I remained guarded about my response to his work: I did not like the morality, the I-told-you-so tone of much scientific work. What if Bose had been able to prove that plants were indeed living things? What did it imply, or rather, what did he want his discovery to imply? To my rebellious teenage mind at the time, Bose's joyousness at his discoveries sometimes seemed to mirror the inexhaustible enthusiasm of NASA scientists that attended the discovery of some trace of 'life' in space, on planets or satellites. But long years of living with the idea of Bose, and in many ways also living Bose's life, had made me experience the true nature of his scientific curiosity. Plants were 'living things' because plants were living things, just as a poem was a poem and the moon was the moon—no morality needed to attend such knowledge.

In a way, then, Bose was at heart only a child interested in secrets, in the hidden, in inner lives. I could relate to that urge, having experienced it often: didn't the tree feel exhausted on a hot day in May, didn't the tree feel sad to see leaves fall at its root, didn't it feel jealous when its neighbour was given more water than it, and so on. But most of all, the secret I wanted to know was how young plants felt when their parent died? Did they feel like orphans? Bose was not just keen on discovering the secrets for himself; he wanted the plants to tell us their own secrets. In that, the instruments he designed were like lie detector units.

'The secret of plant life was thus for the first time revealed by the autographs of the plant itself. This evidence of the plant's own script removed the longstanding error which divided the vegetable world into sensitive and insensitive,' Bose declared to the world in a lecture in the winter of 1917. It wouldn't be far-fetched to read this as the joy of a parent who had, at last, succeeded in proving to the world that his child was 'normal' because it had 'spoken', for above all things, movement and speech seemed to be the primary definition of life for Bose. In this he couldn't be faulted because that had been the accusation against plants for centuries—they did not move. Bose's favourite example of such movement came from his hometown: 'The remarkable performance of the Praying Palm Tree of Faridpore, which bows, as if to prostrate itself, every evening, is only one of the latest instances which show that the supposed insensibility of plants and still more of rigid trees is to be ascribed to wrong theory and defective observation. My investigations show that all plants, even the trees, are fully alive to changes of environment; they respond visibly to all stimuli, even to the slight fluctuations of light caused by a drifting cloud.'

Bose notes the similarities in the effect poison has on plant and animal life, and then cites a remarkable example that gives away his indefatigable belief in the plant-person equivalence: 'A plant carefully protected under glass from outside shocks, looks sleek and flourishing; but its higher nervous function is then found to be atrophied. But when a succession of blows is rained on this effete and bloated specimen, the shocks themselves create nervous channels and arouse anew the deteriorated nature. And is it not shocks of adversity and not cotton-wool protection that evolve true manhood?' I had to read that twice, just to be sure that Bose was comparing a plant protected from the harshness of the environment with a man who had kept himself away from life's weathering. It is also not difficult to see how Bose is resisting the infantilization of plants here, a minor irony given his own tendency to treat them as children, his children.

'At Cambridge,' Bose reported in a speech delivered to the students of Calcutta's Presidency College, 'the undergraduates in the class of plant-physiology came to me and made fun of the supposed inaptitude of our countrymen for accurate scientific observation.' He credits this insult as a propellant to his furious desire to articulate the secret lives of plants. 'Perhaps it was that sub-conscious impression, lying dormant for many years, which turned the course of my investigations to reveal the inner history of the inarticulate life of plants.' In the famous essay titled 'Automatism in Plant and Animal', published in the *Modern Review* in 1908, Bose begins by talking about the response of plants to light, to poison, to heat and cold, and in all these cases, he draws comparisons with the human body, most often with the human heart. Then he begins describing the behaviour of Desmodium, the telegraph plant, 'whose pulsation goes on perpetually, like the human heart'—Bose cut off the supply of food and light to the plant and restored it to favourable conditions again. When he begins to explain its behaviour, Bose unconsciously lapses into comparing the plant with a child: 'One notices the same phenomenon in any healthy body, after it has been fed. From a state of quiescence before feeding, it will afterwards throw out its limbs again and again in a rhythmic manner, expressive of overflowing energy. This is also seen in children of a larger growth, when an intensely pleasurable stimulation will cause them to "dance for joy".' And then, almost instantaneously,

Bose turns the plant-children into tree-adults and the physiological to the psychological: 'This multiple rhythmic response is not improbably the expression of an overflowing self-esteem or egotism!'

One can only estimate my joy in becoming aware of these comparisons, not just his thinking of plants as his human children but also the easy fluidity with which he saw the workings of two seemingly very different species, the plant and the human, as here: 'There is no more difficulty in understanding this process in the plant, though maintained in opposition to the attracting power of gravity, than in understanding the peristaltic action of the human body. We may thus regard the channels of the ascent of sap in the plant as a sort of diffuse heart.' He notes the similarities between the human response to light and compares it immediately with the plant—light is food for both, and then Bose moves to the most difficult, even controversial, area of his study. He demands obedience from his plants, he wants to hear or read them speak. And again he turns the plants into children: 'It is comparatively easy to make a rebellious child obey: to extort answers from plants is indeed a problem!' And he becomes nanny: 'By many years of close contiguity, however, I have some understanding of their ways.' Guilt follows, analogous to a strict teacher who is bent on making his pupils speak: 'I take the opportunity to make public confession of various acts of cruelty which I have from time to time perpetrated on unoffending plants, in order to compel them to give me answers.'

To read Bose, to live like him, is to become aware of a liberating sense of life where one can be plant and human at the same time. As a night owl who hates mornings for the permanently violent abruptness with which they inaugurate the working day, this one is my favourite: 'Amongst plants, as with ourselves, there is, very early in the morning, especially after a cold night, a certain sluggishness.' There are similarities in day time behaviour too: 'In the excessive heat of mid-day, again, though the first few answers are very distinct, yet fatigue soon sets in. On a stormy day, the plant remains obstinately silent.' And this: 'In summer it takes *Mimosa* ten to fifteen minutes to recover from a blow, whereas in winter the same thing would take over half an hour. In all this, you will recognize the similarity between human response and that of the plant.' Bose records the 'nervous' behaviour of plants and posits them against the human. Like a lover, like a parent, he wants some sign of communication that will tell him that they are aware of his existence, of his affection: he looks for 'spontaneity' in plant behaviour. He'd be happy with just that acknowledgement, but it doesn't come in any 'normal' way for there is no 'conversation' after all.

A plant's—like a human's—last answer to stimuli is the response to death. And so Bose asks: 'How does the plant then give this last answer?' For this too, he had created an instrument, to record a plant's 'last words' as it were: 'In the script of the Morograph, or Death-recorder, the line that up to this point was being drawn, becomes suddenly reversed, and then ends. This is the last answer of the plant.' I know this line ought to have made me sad, given the number of times I have been inconsolable after the death of a plant, especially saplings, but instead I find myself chuckling: 'Morograph', the name of the instrument, comes from 'moro', the Bangla word for death. This portmanteau word might have made the dying plants laugh too, if only they could. But they wouldn't—laugh or cry.

And hence the ultimate frustration, the lack of dialogue in this relationship, the need to know how the one you love feels about you. Bose is speaking for plant lovers like me when he says, 'If the plant could have been made thus to keep its own diary, then the whole of its history might have been recovered!' It must have been this pent up frustration that led Jagadish Bose to name his collection of essays *Awbyakto*, meaning the 'unsaid' in Bangla. The similarity is easy to spot—Bose as plant, speaking for his offspring, trying to articulate the unsaid. This silence of the unspoken seemed to be a leitmotif of his life. His famous essay, 'Gachher Kawtha', could mean two things— 'The Story of Plants'; and also 'What Plants Say'. Bose begins with the fundamental question that plagued him all his life: 'Do plants say something?' Impatient with their lack of speech comprehensible to humans, he begins by criticizing our over-privileging of human speech over what might be considered tree speech. Bose refuses to believe that silence could also be a tree dialect, and annoyed with this one-sided communication, he almost scolds them for behaving like children: 'Have plants never spoken? Is it true that only man can articulate his thoughts most clearly? And those who can't speak *clearly*, aren't their words not speech? We have a child who can't speak very clearly—he can say only a few words, but even those aren't clear enough... But we can understand what he is trying to say...his eyes, his face and the movements of his hands and head tell us what he's trying to say though others don't get him.' I begin to see a semblance of truth behind the caretaker Mr Rai's words—this seamless conflation between plants and children.

Was this true, then, that childless or childfree people tend to think of plants as their babies? Bose refers to seeds as eggs, he spends a lot of energy on talking about the 'mother' tree's altruism, and in the next essay in the book, titled *Udbhid-er Jawnmo O Mrityu* ('The Birth and Death of Plants'), he likens the young sapling to an infant: 'The seed is hiding below the soil... It seems someone is calling the child from outside, "Don't sleep anymore, climb up to the top, come see the sunlight..." Have you seen a germinating seed? It looks exactly like an infant raising its head to see this new world with wonder and surprise.'

What was it about plants that made parents out of people like Bose and me? It wasn't all my fault for Bose's clarifications led me on: 'Plants eat the way we eat. We have teeth and can therefore eat hard things. Infants don't have teeth; they can only drink milk. Plants don't have teeth either; that is why they can only eat or drink water or water like fluids or water.' In a flash a scene from my childhood appeared to me: Standard Three; Nature Study class; I stand up from my seat and tell the teacher, 'My lower tooth has become loose'; 'It's your milk tooth, a new adult tooth will grow again.' In the weekly test on seed germination, I wrote, 'The seed then loses its milk teeth and gradually grows into an adult.'

It wasn't only in the way plants ate or drank that Bose found them childlike. Take the way we fetishize or feel affection for baby hands and baby feet just because they happen to be small. Bose writes in exactly the same manner about leaves: 'Leaves have several tiny mouths. If one looks closely, one would find tiny lips.' And then he writes about

Sumana Roy

plant hunger: the way suckling infants turn towards a mother's breasts, plants turn towards light: 'The primary instinct of plants is to feed on light.' Bose then succumbs to flat anthropomorphism, an emotion I recognize well from having experienced it all too often: 'Seeds are a plant's children... When a plant is covered with flowers, it seems that the plant is smiling... What shines through in this beauty is the maternal love of the plant.' A little later, talking about their life cycle and the technology of love in it, Bose writes, 'The plant nurtures the seed with all its sap without caring for its own life... Now the dry plant cannot withstand even a light breeze anymore. It shivers in the wind... Then, having sacrificed its life for its child, the plant dies.'

In another essay a few pages later, the old ambition shows up again. All of us who have loved infants and wanted to know what goes on in their minds will recognize it immediately. We must get plants to write out their thoughts on paper, says Bose in this essay in Bangla. I paraphrase: There are so many countries and so many languages; why not a language of plants then? I concede that the civilized would be annoyed with this proposition, but there is no way out. And so Bose continues—it is a terribly passionate piece of writing, and even the cynic would be moved by his desire to have a plant write its own 'autograph', and then an autobiography. Until this line arrives: 'It's our good fortune that the plant script is pretty close to the Devanagiri—it is difficult for the illiterate or the half literate to decipher.' I have to confess that even I, with all my strange ambitions about plants and my relationship with them, hadn't ever entertained such a thought though I had once wanted to know whether there was a pause, a caesura, a space bar, between plant 'words', or whether it ran non-stop in a long sequence, like the unpredictable length of a child's cry.

Bose's frustration and disappointment is with the 'silence', the lack of reciprocal communication, his need for a dialogue with plants. So conditioned are we to a back-and-forth system of speaking that we do not realize that there could be alternative models of communication as well. The essay 'Nirbak Jeebon', The Silent Life, begins with this tautology: The life around us is terribly silent. And then the old desperation—we have to get plants to tell us their own life stories.

These histories must not be mediated by man, they must come to us directly. Bose's insistence on the 'direct speech' of plants, without man's 'prejudiced intentionality', when it prefaces his comparison between plants and infants, wouldn't strike us as crazy if we think of the many times philosophers, linguists, and brain scientists have wanted to get inside the minds of infants and toddlers to become aware of their thoughts. That is also the reason why all 'histories of childhood', like the histories of plants and trees, are incomplete.

'Torulipi', the script of plants—Bose even had a name for it. After telling us about a stringed instrument which could also double as a writing machine, Bose asks this question in a subheading: Are plants shy? He explains where his question is coming from—only the shy don't respond to our probing after all, just as plants don't verbally. What seems to hurt him the most is not that plants don't speak to him but that they cannot articulate their hurt—Bose ends up equating them with the deaf and dumb. The definition of life is a living creature's immediate response to physical hurt. His questions don't end: does hurt excite a plant? How does a plant communicate its hurt to the rest of the world? How can that piece of communication be recorded? Will that record on paper give us a history of the plant?

And so Bose sets out to map this history of hurt by pinching and torturing his plants and recording their reactions on his different instruments. 'A slight hurt causes only a slight disturbance; the pen moves upwards slightly...a greater hurt causes a longer line.' And then the plants become his children again: 'It takes at least half an hour for a plant to recover from that hurt... Just as there is no guarantee that children would grow taller and wiser after being beaten by a schoolmaster's cane, similarly plants stop growing after being hurt. In both cases, in fact, the growth is hampered.' It was disturbing to read what this great lover of plants had to make the objects of his love undergo in order to reveal their secrets to him. I had the sense of the plants being placed in a prison, a court of law or an inquisition chamber. It made me sad to think why the thought of a hospital for plants had not struck him after his guilt.

⁂

Sumana Roy

Jagadish Bose's mountain house in Darjeeling, now turned into a museum holding a record of his living habits, revealed nothing remarkable about him except that he was a man of educated taste. The wooden walls and floors, now only polished by time, not human hands, held nothing about this ancestry of love, his long romance with the plant world.

As I walked down the steep sloping path from the mountain house, I tripped a few times. The mind remembers but the body forgets easily—my feet and legs had forgotten the resistance offered by steep gradients to their movement. And then I fell. I wasn't hurt, only my ego was dented—which adult likes to fall down against his will? But when the paternal voice of Mr Rai, who was following, told me to be careful because 'women should be careful...miscarriage and all that', I was suddenly angry.

I turned to look at him, hoping my gaze would show him how inappropriate his comments were.

It did not. In fact, his words continued to flow, now adopting the idiom that he perhaps considered appropriate: 'The tree has to be strong. How will it bear fruits otherwise?'

What Jagadish Bose had said in a lecture to the students of Presidency College came to my mind immediately: 'Our motto shall be "We sow though we may not reap the fruit".'

If Bose had been alive, I might have asked him whether plants had any mechanism to abort children they did not need.

GARDENS AND ADULTERY

Lovers no longer
need gardens as they move
into sex in
odd places with
bad names, cosy
under their own
trees. (Mangesh Naik, 'Birds Love')

Towards the end of Satyajit Ray's short telefilm, *Pikoo*, the little boy
Pikoo calls out to his mother from the garden. A little while ago, he has
been given a packet of sketch pens and a drawing book by his mother's
lover. To get rid of him from the scene, his mother has invented a
new game: he must draw all the flowers in their garden using the
appropriate colour from his new pack of colour pens. Though he tells
his old and ailing grandfather that his parents have fought the previous
night, there is a tension in the air that the little boy cannot understand.
What Pikoo doesn't know is that his father has found out about his
mother's 'boyfriend'—while leaving for office and adjusting the knot
of his tie in the mirror, he has dropped the question innocently, 'Isn't
your boyfriend coming today? I found his hair on my pillow. That
strand of hair wasn't mine.'

Pikoo's mother keeps this a secret from her lover until he arrives,
carrying a bribe of colour pens for his lover's young son. But even
this discovery of being discovered cannot keep their bodies from each
other. Pikoo, of course, is too young to know all this—he is happy to be
bribed. The servants (there are quite a few of them in this upper middle-

class household, with its huge house and a sprawling, well-maintained, manicured garden) are playing a game of cards, Pikoo's grandfather is on the verge of suffering from what would be a third and fatal heart attack. Pikoo, the painter with newly found colours, has painted red flowers, then yellow marigolds, a red fireball, and then a pink lotus. But when he finds the white frangipani flowers on a tree and white lotuses floating on a tiny pond in their garden, he calls out to his mother: 'Ma, I have to draw the white flowers with black ink because there is no white colour in the box.' Ray's camera follows the direction of the sound, moving from the little boy in the garden and climbing into the bedroom of his mother in the first storey of the house where she and her lover are in bed. Ray shows us only the upper torsos in a state of undress, the man on top of the woman. The mother wants to break away from the embrace—black being used to paint white flowers, the innocent proposition of her young son has turned into a moral for her. Her lover is annoyed—he is only body, his time and bribe are wasted, he complains. A drop of rain falls on little Pikoo's drawing book. It changes nearly everything—lotuses float on water; in Pikoo's new world, water changes the colour of the lotus from white to smudged black. Soon Pikoo will discover that his grandfather has died while he was drawing flowers in the garden. It is a short film, remarkable if only for the way Ray uses two 'things' which are attached to innocence—the little boy and flowers, and their interchangeability, flower as child and vice versa; the relationship between children and adultery, its temporary determination and its short, obese life. The question about black used to paint white, and the philosophical and moral narratives they propel, gain substance because of their attachment to something as 'innocent' as flowers. This is, of course, not the first time Ray is using the space of the garden to emplot adultery. Though—and because—it is so much more than that, the iconic scene of Charulata on the swing in her garden is another. Arunava Sinha translates this Tagore novella along with two others in the collection *Three Women*. Whether it's Charulata in *The Broken Nest*, the sisters Sharmila and Urmimala in *The Two Sisters* or Neeraja in *The Arbour*, we find Rabindranath Tagore employing the garden motif in all three novellas.

Charulata first. The lonely, sentimental, affectionate, creative and imaginative woman who is married to the wealthy newspaper editor Bhupati, but feels emotionally closer to her brother-in-law, the young poet Amal. Their relationship is built over literature and a garden as we see in this excerpt from *The Broken Nest*:

> To dub the plot of land that lay behind Bhupati's house a garden would be an exaggeration. The primary vegetation of this so-called garden was an ambarella tree.
>
> Charu and Amal had set up a committee for the development of this plot. Together they had conjured up the garden of their dream with diagrams and plans.
>
> 'Bouthan, you must water the plants in our garden yourself like the princesses of yore,' said Amal.
>
> 'And we'll have a hut there...' added Charu.
>
> ...Amal drew a map of the garden with great ceremony, using paper and pencil, ruler and compass. Together they drew up some two dozen maps, recreating their vision each day... Initially the plan was that Charu would use some of her monthly stipend to build the garden gradually; Bhupati never spared a glance for anything that went on at home, when the garden was ready they would give him a big surprise. He would think they had used Aladdin's lamp to transplant an entire garden from Japan.
>
> ...The plan was to get seeds of cloves from Mauritius, of sandalwood from Karnat, and of cinnamon from Ceylon, but when Amal proposed replacing them with seeds of everyday Indian and English plants from the local market, Charu looked glum. 'Then I don't want a garden,' she said. This was not the way to lower expenses. It was impossible for Charu to curb her imagination alongside the estimate, and no matter what he said, it wasn't acceptable to Amal either.
>
> 'Then, bouthan, you'd better discuss the garden with dada—he's certain to give you money for it.'
>
> 'You and I will make the garden together. There's no fun if I tell him. He might just order an Eden Garden from some English

gardener—where will our plan be then?'

...The great pleasure and glory of all their schemes was that it was limited to just themselves.

After much misunderstanding and a series of events that take Amal away from her, Charulata is left to her own—neither her husband, the newspaper editor Bhupathi, nor her brother-in-law, can fathom the depth of despair and desolation of this childless woman. Like the garden that is never built except as a fantasy dialogue, Charu's thoughts, her guilt, her inability to 'forget in that distant land a wife who dreams of another man', turn her into a room without walls. It is striking that Tagore employs a metaphor from plant life to talk about her in the end: 'a frightened beast pursued by a forest fire'. From a garden to a forest fire is indeed a long journey.

Like Charulata, Sharmila in *Two Sisters* 'had not had a child, had probably given up hope of having one'. After her husband acquires a house in Bhawanipur, Sharmila's 'self-sacrifice, so palpable once, now showed itself indirectly: in decorating the house, in maintaining the garden...in the blue crystal flower vase on the corner of the desk in his office which held marigolds'. On 14 November, 'Shashanka's birthday and the most important occasion in Sharmila's life', 'their home was decorated specially with flowers'. Sharmila falls ill with an obscure disease, and Urmi, her younger sister, comes to stay with her, to look after her and also to become a supervisor of the domestic machinery at work in her sister's household. Tagore uses the fruit-flower trope to show how Sharmila begins to see herself in her sister, as if it were a natural progression, the relationship between fruits of the same tree: 'When Urmi peeled and sliced apples with her lovely hands, when she arranged the orange slices...when she broke open a pomegranate... Sharmila seemed to see herself in her sister.' Gradually Sharmila begins to see that Urmi's childishness has endeared her to Shashanka, and then the terrible realization: 'Now I know, as I'm about to die, that whatever else I may have achieved, I haven't succeeded in making him happy... She has not taken my place, I cannot take hers. My going may hurt him but her going will mean he'll lose everything.' But Urmi is betrothed to Nirad, a scholar with austere and abstract philosophies of living. And there are many shades of grey in their relationship. 'Urmi was like a tree clinging to the earth but deprived of light, its leaves robbed of colour. She became impatient at times, wondering why the man couldn't even write her a proper letter.' If Urmi is an unhappy tree, Sharmila is a 'goddess' deserving of flowers, even if they are plucked from her own garden.

Shashanka, her husband, had got a portrait of hers 'framed at a foreign store in great style and hung it on the wall of his office directly opposite his chair. The gardener put fresh flowers in the vase before it, every day'. Here is the emergence of a binary—the flowers, severed from life, put in a vase for the wife Sharmila; and flowers blooming in the garden for the sister-in-law Urmimala. When they make plans to go out, Shashanka suggests the circus, Urmi chooses the Botanical Gardens. 'Eventually, while showing Urmi how well the sunflowers were blooming in the garden, Shashanka suddenly took her hand, saying, 'I'm sure you know that I am in love with you. And as for your sister, she's a goddess...' In the end, however, Tagore privileges the flowers in the vase over the 'flowers blooming in the garden', the inside over the outside. The sister-in-law leaves, and Shashanka, who suddenly discovers that his business has gone bankrupt, returns to his wife, becoming a debtor for life.

The third novella in the collection, *The Arbour*, has this epigraph: 'She had been banished from the very garden that had claimed her heart, the heart of the childless mother. It was such a cruel separation...' This is a story about a childless couple, Aditya and Neeraja. 'Aditya had made a name for himself in the flower trade. In their marriage, Neeraja and her husband had come together through tending to the garden. The flowers and blossoms, with their ever-changing loveliness, had always renewed their joy in each other. Just as the émigré awaits letters from friends back home on the days when the special post arrives, so too did they await, from season to season, the welcome of their flowers and plants.'

Neeraja is unwell now, a curse Tagore seems to reserve for several childless women in his fiction, and when the novella begins, we find her looking out of the window, to the orchid room, the garden below, the 'flowering vines wound around its pickets'. 'A brass pitcher in another corner held a bunch of tuberose flowers, their faint fragrance floating in the heavy air.' It is as if Charulata, Sharmila and Neeraja, women without children, need to fill their lives with the equivalent of children—in Tagore's world that would be flowers. These women are, with their affluent husband's indulgence, rather like children themselves.

I spoke to Arunava Sinha, the translator of these novellas, and asked him why he had chosen these three among the many that Tagore had written. It was the theme of adultery running through them, he said. In that, the 'three' of the 'Three Women' in the title was a mischievous joke—there were more than three women in the three stories. How else would there be adultery? For this is the mathematics of romantic relationships. Marriage is an arithmetic of one plus one. It rejects the notion of surplus. Yes, other organisms attach themselves to this joint enterprise—house, children, relatives, plans, and quite often, gardens. But they remain props. It is only the entry of another human adult into the room of the marriage that disturbs its equilibrium.

Is that why Tagore moves the space of adultery from inside the house to the controlled wilderness of the garden? But in these novellas, it is not adultery alone which needs the garden. It is the fact of the 'three women' being childless. In Tagore, gardening is made the most 'natural' substitute for child-rearing. These women of leisure, occasional but devoted readers of novels in their mother tongue Bangla, with wealthy and busy husbands, ill (perhaps from loneliness and depression, though Tagore never makes that clear), become passionate, second-hand gardeners. Because readers like to think of their favourite writers as a wondrous mix of the diagnosis and the cure, I had come to Tagore to ask whether my obsessive interest in plant life too came from my childlessness.

Here is Tagore in *The Arbour*:

Everyone had lost hope of Neeraja having a child. They had given Ganesh a place to live in their establishment, and just as his young son was beginning to stir Neeraja's thwarted maternal passion—the boy reeling under its relentless onslaught—she became pregnant. The mother's soul *flowered* within her, the horizon ahead glowed pink in the dawn of new life; *sitting beneath a tree* Neeraja busied herself stitching clothes for the new born, producing a hundred different patterns. (italics mine)

Neeraja, now seriously ill, and her husband had once been partners in gardening, parents as it were in the nurture of plants. It is interesting to see her read the barometer of their relationship through flowers: 'For the first time he forgot my regular morning flowers. I'll get worse day by day,' she complains about her husband. 'Before starting his work for the day, Aditya always left a hand-picked flower by his wife's bedside. Neeraja had waited for it every single day. And now Aditya had chosen to send the day's special flower with Sarala.'

Neeraja does not like Sarala, her husband's cousin and new helper in the garden. Ill and terribly dependent on people, the only way she can insult this other woman is through her knowledge of botany.

'Do you know the name of this flower?' Neeraja asked needlessly, a little later.
Sarala could easily have said she didn't, but her pride was hurt, so she answered, 'Amaryllis.'
'Fat lot you know!' Neeraja cut her down in unfair rage. 'It's called Grandiflora.'
'Maybe,' answered Sarala softly.
'What do you mean maybe? It is! Are you suggesting I'm wrong?'
Sarala knew Neeraja had deliberately used an incorrect name to register her protest; needling someone else to forget her own hurt.

Time and again, Tagore resurrects the same metaphor, the alignment of mothering and gardening. 'She had been banished from the very garden—so near and yet so far—that had claimed the heart, the heart of the childless mother.' When Ramen, her husband's cousin, comes to visit her, he calls her a 'forest goddess', and Neeraja asks him to marry Sarala, blessing him with these words: 'May the goddess of your garden be bound to your breast forever...'

As if to remind his readers that this wedding of metaphors is not his invention, Tagore invokes the tradition of thought about women and flowers in Aditya's voice: 'In ancient times trees used to flower at the touch of women's feet, flowers used to bloom at a taste of the shower from their lips; my garden has returned to the era of Kalidasa. Flowers have bloomed, in all their myriad hues, on either side of the path on which you walk, the rose garden is drunk on the wine you've sprinkled in the spring breeze... Without you this heaven of flowers would have been overrun by the invasion of monstrous traders. How fortunate for me that you are the queen of my heavenly arbour.'

There are, of course, different kinds of gardeners: 'Meshomashai knew how to grow flowers, not how to grow a business,' Aditya tells Sarala about her father. But there are other kinds too, and their relationships to their gardens are more emotional. Neeraja pleads with her husband: 'I maintain that the orchid room is just yours and mine, she has no right to be there. Give her your entire garden if you really want to; just keep a tiny part of it dedicated to my memory alone. Surely I can stake this small claim after so many years together.' Just before this, Aditya had been telling his wife about his uncle's—Sarala's father's—interest in orchids, that 'he sent people off to get him orchids from the Celebes, Java, even from China', and that his daughter, Sarala, therefore, 'understands them even better than I do.' I think it is significant that Tagore aligns Sarala with the orchid, which continues to be an 'exotic' flower in mainstream discourse. The 'Other' woman must belong to that tradition, as it were.

Aditya is stunned by Neeraja's pain, and he begins to see that he has been responsible for this—his unqualified praise for Sarala's talent in gardening has triggered his wife's jealousy so that she 'would look up unusual names of obscure flowers in English books; she would then ask Sarala to identify them, and when Sarala got one wrong, laugh uproariously.' Tagore orchestrates the geometry of adultery through the tropes of plant life. So, the husband and wife show possessiveness—over each other, and the marriage—through their proprietorship of the garden.

'Don't cry anymore, Neeru, tell me what I should do. Do you want Sarala not to be involved in the garden?'

Snatching her hand away, Neeraja said, 'Nothing, I want nothing, it's your garden...'

'Neeru, how could you say it's my garden alone. Isn't it yours too? When did we become separated from each other?'

'...How will this broken spirit of mine allow me to stand up to your amazing Sarala? Where do I have the power to look after you, to take care of your garden?'

The bittersweet arguments continue until Aditya makes the fantastic declaration that if it is adultery—the entry of a third person into the marital space—that is disturbing Neeraja, then he should have considered the garden his 'rival in love': 'Since we've been married, I have come to realize that your garden is as precious to you as your heart; I considered the garden no different from myself ever since. Or else I'd have quarrelled bitterly with your garden and I'd never have been able to bear it. It would have been my rival in love. You know how I have merged it within myself. How I have become one with it... Is the garden any less than my body?'

Is the garden any less than my body?

But none of this affects his wife who says: 'Because you love her more than you love me.'

That Neeraja's words are not untrue is evident in the next chapter where, after Ramen has tried his best to woo Sarala, Aditya tells her about his feelings for her, employing the figure of the garden again: 'Is there a shovel on this planet that can dig those days out of the earth? ...What lay concealed in the bud for twenty-three years is blooming today... Why did I not see you, why did I make the mistake of getting married?' Later, he takes a 'small bunch of rose-coloured chestnut flowers' for Sarala, as if almost in penance.

His wife's grief makes Aditya decide to start a new division in the business, for growing flower and vegetable seeds. 'A house with a garden in Maniktala is available,' he writes in a letter to his wife, and he is 'going to settle Sarala there, in charge of that division'. After a series of misunderstandings, we discover that Sarala has been arrested for entering the chamber of the governor general's room to steal the casket of the governor general's wife while Neeraja is trying her best to get her garden—a near metonymy for her marriage—back into health. 'Are you telling me that my garden should be on a sickbed just because I am?'

A chain of instructions follow: 'Bring the map of the garden to me, and my garden diary... I will stamp the garden before I go... For the next few days this garden is going to be mine, mine alone. Then I will gift this garden of mine to you.' These are the words of a woman who knows that her proprietorship—of her garden, her husband, her marriage, and indeed, of her life—is short. 'You have to remember that it's my garden, mine alone, I shall never give up my rights to it.'

Neeraja wants to live, she asks Aditya about what are only his second-hand experiences of death. Is there nothing about it in his books? And then she turns to her garden: 'It can never happen that the garden will be there and I won't.' Neeraja asks to see Sarala and when the latter arrives, she insists that there is no one else in the room except the two of them. What follows—on the last page of the novella—is quite unpredictable:

> She gripped Sarala's hand tightly, her voice became sharper, she screamed, 'There'll be no room for you, you she-devil, no room for you. I'm staying, I'm staying.'
> The ashen, emaciated figure in her loose chemise suddenly leapt up from her bed. In a contorted voice she screamed, 'Get out, get out of here this instant, else I'll strike at your heart day after day, I'll suck up all your blood.'
> And instantly, she slumped to the floor.
> Aditya ran into the room at the sound of her voice. Emptied of life, Neeraja's last words had by then been silenced forever.

As I closed the book of novellas, two things immediately crossed my mind. The first was *Banchharamer Bagaan* (Banchharam's Garden), a film by Tapan Sinha, that I had watched as a child. Banchharam, an aged gardener, who now owns a large garden of flowers and fruits, will just not die. This, when two generations of father and son, wealthy landlords, both greedy for ownership of the garden, have died and one of them turned into the garden's resident ghost. A greedy grandson lurks nearby, lured by the prospect of owning the garden. But old—ancient—Banchha will just not die. How can he leave this garden, *his* garden? I wondered whether the 'ghost' of Neeraja might come to haunt what was once her garden.

The other thing I thought about was the request I make to my husband from time to time: 'Please look after my plants after I die.' If I had human children, I would have made the same request. But they might have been adults by the time I died, and therefore not really in need of daily attention and care. But my plant children, no matter how old they grew, would always be dependent on someone's altruism for survival. And so I worried for them. In such intense moments of self-scrutiny, I wondered about the future of my 'dead body'.

Would I too, overcome by possessive love, return as caretaker to my plants, a ghost gardener?

Part VII

Lost in the Forest
—Pablo Neruda, '*Lost in the Forest*'

LOST IN THE FOREST

On his first visit to such a large congregation of trees, my three-and-a-half-year-old nephew asked about the name of the place we were in. This is how the conversation went:

'What is the name of this place?'
'It's called a forest.'
'That means we can rest here.'

It takes a child to prise open obvious etymologies of words and expose us to the sharp edges of our chairs. I had never thought of a forest as 'for rest'.

Inside every forest is a little boy lost. We had come to find our little boys.

'In the middle of the forest there's an unexpected clearing that can only be found by those who have gotten lost.' That line is by Tomas Tranströmer. Truth be told, we had come to the forest to get lost. 'Lost' has two different meanings: one in the forest, and another in civilization. The forest seems to inevitably exist as one half of a binary. On the other side is a library or museum, a university or gymnasium—trees versus books as educators. Bibhutibhushan Bandyopadhyay, one of my favourite writers in Bangla, writing in the first half of the twentieth century, recognized this binary and moved between it, in his life as well as his writing. Spending six years between 1924 and 1930 in the forests and uncultivated land of Bihar's Bhagalpur district where he was employed as the assistant manager of an estate, Bibhutibhushan grew needy in sharing his experience of being in the forest with those who had been deprived of it. A diary entry of 12 February 1928—he was a sincere diarist and the full-bodied entries are characterized by a delicious curiosity about the secretive world of plants and the sky—makes us aware of this desire to write about the forest: 'I will write something about the life in the jungle—rigorous and dynamic, radiant with courage—images of an outcast life. About riding in this lonely forest, losing one's way in the dark paths, living a solitary life in a little shelter...' In Bibhutibhushan I recognize myself. I recognize a relative who had set out to get lost in a forest.

⁕

Why have hermits and thinkers gone to the forest to surrender to its stillness?

I have stood inside a forest, surrounded by its paralysing restfulness, and wondered whether the forest has an ego. I had once been overwhelmed by that ego or whatever it is that directs the forest. It might be prenatal dreams, as a hypnotherapist explained to me, it could also be the clash of human history versus those outside human history, or it could be nothing. The woman in the forest a thousand years ago and I could not be the same person. That there is a connection between forest life and creativity, whether spiritual or intellectual, is no longer questioned. 'The forests await the little boy who will become the artist,' writes Bibhutibhushan in *Smritir Lekha*, his diary notes from Bhagalpur, in August 1925. What is it about the forest air that no artist has bothered to investigate and no entrepreneur bothered to bottle and sell?

Aranyak takes its title from the *Aranyakas*, the Books of the Forests in the Vedas. As the translator Rimli Bhattacharya reminds us in a prefatory note, 'The destruction of the forest is a necessary prelude in the Adiparva of the Mahabharata: Khandava vana is consumed by fire to provide a clearing for Indraprastha whose urbane magnificence is only the site of further dissension. In Indian literary texts, the period spent in the forest constitutes the locale of numerous aranya parvas (forest episodes) as either exile, voluntary or enforced, a temporary sojourn, or interlude as also the space to which householders finally retire.'

For me this was the real mystery about forest life. How had

humans turned the forest into both nest and cage, pampering and punishment? The well-educated Calcutta-bred Bengali man in *Aranyak* had been able to discover himself only by living in the forest; in the epics Ramayana and Mahabharata, for instance, Rama, accompanied by his wife and brother, goes to the forest for his exile, as do the five Pandava brothers and their wife Draupadi, this state of living called 'vanvas' (van: forest; vas: living); young male students spent more than a decade of their lives learning statecraft and warfare, language, logic and philosophy from their gurus in the teacher's tapovan, forest hermitage; then there was the Vanaprastha, when people who had crossed the age of fifty were expected to lead a semi-retired life in the forest. As a child who had visited forests only for winter picnics, I imagined this to be some version of punishment for I expected forest living to be full of hardship, and also meant only for the poor, given it was the homeless I encountered on those outings, waiting expectantly to be fed as soon as we'd finished our quota of eating and wasting. How could such a hard life, one deprived of familiar comforts, be expected to yield rich results?

There is something about the forest that makes it analogous to a dream.

Connected to this is the wonder and beauty surrounding the moonlit forest. As a child, I'd called a moonlit forest an 'X-ray forest', an anecdote my mother continues to mention with late pride to our relatives. That feeling has stayed with me—this awareness of the bluish moonlight tearing unnecessary membranes away from sight so that when one is inside the forest, one feels privy to a secret, some code that brings the inner and interior life of the trees out into the open, like a séance or even a short-lived presentation of the forest's intestines on a surgical table.

When Satya, the protagonist of *Aranyak*, encounters the forest on moonlit nights, there is immediate alchemy. 'There is one day I shall never forget... As I stood beneath the moonlit skies on that still silent night, I felt that I had chanced upon an unknown fairy kingdom. No mortal would come here to work. Places such as these, bereft of human beings, became the sporting ground for fairies—I had not done well to enter without permission.' People like to think of the forest as a patched green quilt, but I know that the colour of the forest is blue. On a moonlit night it is this that rises to the surface. And it is this that makes it a relative of the sky, not a mirror image but a kinship, the way one parent is related to another, not by blood but by relation and responsibility. Not green but blue is the colour of this wonder and magic. I still remember my childhood word for the forest air, a coinage that married my newfound science with wonder: 'Blue Oxygen'. There is something about the forest coming alive under a full moon. One of Rabindranath's most popular songs is about the same sense of exhilaration—'Jochhna raatey shawbai gyachhey bon-ay', Everyone's gone to the forest on this full-moon night. Satya writes, 'And each time, I have felt that while I was in Bengal I had not known that moonlight could be so exquisite, that it could evoke such fear and detachment—the only words for which would be *udaas*.' Is this why we go to the forest then? To pamper the finest strain of melancholy, to tune the refined sadness inside us? Is the moonlit forest an emotion then?

'I was in the midst of a terrifying isolation...now, when the moon was full it was as though I was travelling through an unknown fairyland, beautiful and mysterious.' Satya had not looked for exile or solitude—he was far too young to feel the need for either, but now that he found himself amidst it, he felt crippled by loneliness, which was, to him then, as it continues to be to many of us now, the religion of the forest. I saw Satya's education by the forest and I grew nervous about the possibility of similar feelings of exhaustion growing in me. But I soon realized that I was a more advanced student compared to Satya—his primary education in the forest is in solitude, a lesson I had sought and mastered to my satisfaction. The loneliness inside a forest must be different from other genres of loneliness. Why else would Satya and many after him, like the man in this popular Adhunik Bangla song, feel it in such an agonizing and yet beautiful manner? 'Bonotawl phooley phooley dhaka'—the forest floor is covered with flowers, the moonlight washes the singer and the forest in luxurious measure, and yet the rhetorical question, 'Bhalo ki laagey?' Is it possible to like this?

And hence the question—why is the forest so linked with solitude? I taught Thoreau's *Walden* to my students, and every few days one of us wondered—can there be a solitary tree in a forest? Is a solitary tree a lonely tree? And if one is not lonely, where is companionship to be found in a forest?

Along with solitude is the education in silence. Like the whispering sibilants that make relatives of 'solitude' and 'silence', the Bangla words for each also tell of a similar story of dependence—'nirjawn', without people, uninhabited, and 'nistawbdho', without a sound. Both require training—Satya, like all of us, has been educated in the opposite, sound and noise, and their source, people and crowds. 'Imagine a peculiar silence enveloping the entire forest land. A silence that may not be imagined until you have experienced it.'

My disenchantment with the ambition industry and the violence of professional success had brought me here. My hopelessly romantic need to live like a tree, with other trees in a forest, had guided me to this imagined communitarianism where self-containment and a related self-contentment were the abiding ethic. There was physical hardship, yes, but there was little psychological warfare. I had no illusions about the expansive ambitions that the forest shared with the city: both were fuelled by the greed for territorialization, both were superb encroachers when left to their own, and both needed easy converts. And so the need for parasites in the worlds of both the forest and the city.

But it was the differences that had brought me to the forest. Do forests have nationalities? Bibhutibhushan seems to have discovered the meaninglessness of these nationalist and exclusionist categories in the forest. These forest dwellers—and this included all plant life resident inside it—did not know who or where Bharatvarsha was. Only one kind of warfare seems to be important to the people here. Not a single sound from the freedom struggle against the British enters this space, the war call is against the trees in the jungle—the forest has to give way to agriculture, land must be tamed. There is enthusiasm and there is agony. And so the many moral and linguistic gestures prefixed around forests—deforestation, a sin; afforestation, redemption.

The feeling of an inevitable homelessness when faced with the possibility of getting lost in the forest creeps in on many of us who think of the home as studio, home as theatre, a stage without entry or exit marks, without prompters and permanent residents, home without assignations of rooms based on functionality (bedroom and bathroom and kitchen and so on). This is the first step in the relationship with the forest, into becoming forest-like, as it were, for we gradually become the lovers we take. 'I lost my way one evening on the way back from a survey camp at Ajmabad,' writes Satya of his first experience of getting lost. In a delightful episode in *Pather Panchali*, Apu gets lost in the neighbouring jungle while looking for his elder sister Durga. The fruit trees and the webs of parasitic plants hanging from them become terribly scary to the little boy—he imagines ghosts and monsters and he imagines death like only a child can. It is this viscerality of the forest that has made hunters of men, the desire to tame and conquer what is, in effect, only a congregation of trees. But more importantly perhaps, it is the recognition of the forest as having a mind of its own, the mind of an intelligent competitor who can outwit the human that makes one become an alert animal in the forest. In this, the forest separates the mental age of men—the sportsperson from the hermit, one bringing his body to compete with the forest, the other to bury his old mind and watch it sprout from old ruins.

We have seen it in the forest films, the human face as mirror, reflecting the jungle and its unpredictability. These films hold together as thrillers because most of them are only seeking a way out of the jungle where all the fear and horror are. But, as Satya and Tranströmer tell us, that is exactly the gift of the forest—only here can you get lost. How many places on earth actually remain on earth where one can get lost? In David Wagoner's poem, 'Lost', the forest turns into an active participant in the lost-and-found game.

> Stand still. The trees ahead and bushes beside you
> Are not lost.

The poem is a good reminder of the plant and human difference inside a forest: 'The trees ahead and bushes beside you / Are not lost.' Are the trees not lost because they can't move? Is being lost then only a function of movement? In this, who is the loser, the tree or us?

In a post-GPS age where it is nearly impossible to get lost, and where tourism agencies might even design 'Getting Lost' modules to entertain clients, only one who has got lost in a forest will know that there is no solution to this except getting lost even further. The wise have recognized that, and so they have let the forest become an analogy for the mind, resting on new locations, without a permanent address. Against the stasis of the trees is flow. The lost and found symmetry of our lives, constructed as it is by a vigilant bureaucracy, is subverted by the forest. 'Midway on our life's journey, I found myself / In dark woods, the right road lost.' That is Dante, in Robert Pinsky's translation. This begs the question that I've tried to answer all my life: Is there a 'right road' inside a forest?

'Losing oneself' is a terribly romantic, even elitist, idea. Getting lost in the forest begins as an extension of this idea—I say this as a happy victim. Whenever I've walked into a forest to get lost, I have, without admitting to myself at the time, known that there would be a road leading out of it, one that joins my house with the forest in some possible geometry. This is a bit like the boatman's faith—there must be a bank somewhere for his boat to dock and land. And yet, boats get lost on sea and men have spent nearly their entire lives trying to burrow a path out of the forest. Getting lost in a forest is primarily an outsider's art—men, being creatures of land, will get lost in the sea, but not fishes. And so strangers to the forest come from neighbouring places looking for life and a living, they get lost in the forest and eventually, when they find themselves, it is on the cusp of death. A poor man from Patna had come with the idea of locating forestland where he might cultivate lac, but he loses his way inside the forest, and is assaulted by fierce heat and the lack of water. Wandering—where are the exit doors inside a forest?—left him exhausted. 'He had tried to call out for help. But where was he to find people!'

In this last query is the extension of an important philosophical paradox: 'If a tree falls in a forest and no one is around to hear it, does it make a sound?' George Berkeley, writing in the early eighteenth century, asked this question in *A Treatise Concerning the Principles of Human Knowledge*. Variants of this question have been asked by philosophers and physicists, including Albert Einstein and Niels Bohr—answers have ranged from the scientific explanations of sound and its vibrations to metaphysical speculations on the effect incidents have on worlds outside themselves. If Bibhutibhushan's Bihari man were to die in the forest, would it be death at all? Or another version of getting lost? I've felt it sometimes, the sense of being shadowed or followed, while walking alone in a forest, knowing one is alone and yet not completely alone. Aloneness is perhaps a malady, both cause and state of the illness and it is perhaps this that metamorphoses into the imagined spirits of the forest. The question about being scared of loneliness would not come to the inhabitant of the bachelor pad as often as it does to the wanderer in the forest.

> 'Tell me, don't you mind living here all by yourself? You don't go anywhere, you do nothing...do you like it? Don't you find it monotonous, dull?'
> Jaipal stared at me in some surprise as he replied, 'Why should I mind it, Huzoor? I'm quite well. I don't mind it at all.'

This uneasiness of the social creature, in discovering a fellow human in the forest, one who is indifferent to the varying tempers of neighbourhood that make up the world, is a slightly ironic and limited world view. Who has ever asked the tiger to leave the forest for the enchantments of the zoo? Satya's early discomfort in finding people who have chained their destinies to the forest is contrasted by the lives of those whose world is the forest alone. For a city dweller, migration and travel might be the recipe for difference; for a forest being, difference might not be a demand of the nature of his life at all. I doubt the bird looks for a different coloured sky every morning or the tree a different hued sunlight.

The need for holidays and 'change' is a request for space travel, the appetite for different places. Travel through a forest is often an antiquated version of time travel—accretions of unnoticed history made visible in stumps and trunks of trees, quilts of moss, and most marvellously, in the soil where footprint has mixed with fossil, which is both living and a graveyard without signs. Rousseau's rather avuncular dictum of going back to nature might only have meant going to the forest, to live the uncomplicated life of our ancestors, a version of time travel. It is this timelessness of the forest, where Satya can see a mythico-historical figure like Krishna or imagine the river Yamuna in the middle of a severe drought, that has often turned every forest into a possible Vrindavan. 'Vrinda' is, of course, tulsi, the holy basil, sacred to Hindu worship, known to possess great medicinal value, and 'van' is forest. Associated with the birth and childhood of Krishna, his relationship with Radha, and home to several legends and tales about him, Vrindavan was lost to the world until its discovery by Chaitanya Mahaprabhu in the early sixteenth century, when the mystic saint set out to trace and locate sites associated with the life of Krishna. Charles R. Brooks, in his book, *The Hare Krishnas in India*, writes about how 'the ideal state of mind which is properly the goal of every Krishna bhakta is also called Vrindavan'. This is a good pointer to what exactly one finds in a forest, Vrindavan or not, Krishna bhakt or not.

THE RELIGION OF THE FOREST

The forest as a 'state of mind' is perhaps the religion of every dendrophile, a cult of people who feel changed and converted by spending time in a forest. There is a lovely word for it in Japanese: 'shinrin-yoku', forest bathing, or being bathed by a forest; its meaning is so terribly poetic that even mentioning the word seems like a moment changing experience. Is Krishna's romantic playfulness, his wisdom, his extraordinary powers of empathy, his sense of comradeship, and even his insightful statecraft a product of the forest? We are, in spite of our lack of education about the anthropological origins of various institutionalized religions, intuitively aware of the difference in the temperament and teachings of forest religions versus, say, desert religions. The little boy being nurtured by the forest is a tale with many versions—sometimes that boy is Tarzan, sometimes Mowgli, at other times Krishna. I cannot help noticing that all of these are boys growing up without their biological parents. The forest as parent in one's childhood turns to the teacher and later, with the accumulation of dead skin on soles of feet, an unlikely dependent. The forest needs me as much as I need the forest. The symbiotic nature of this need took me years to comprehend. In the Sukna Forest at the foothills of the Eastern Himalayas, for instance, I felt wondrously happy and calmed but also guilty, this for years, for I felt like an interloper who was disturbing the forest during its sleeping hours. That is the sense I always had as a child—when asked to imagine Kumbhakarna, Ravana's brother from the epic who slept for half the year and ate gluttonously during the other half, I inevitably ended up imagining the demon—a man—as a sleepy forest. A waking forest would be a calamity, I was certain.

Moving in the forest was like playing with a parent's body as he or she slept—I moved around secretively, hoping not to be caught in the middle of some mischief. Waking would lead to the end of the game and also possible punishment. Every sound was a call to alert, every step a trap. These two lives—faces, personalities—of the forest seemed so contradictory to me that I did not know what to make of them. There were the forest literature and films that almost never interested me—there was too much busyness in the world outside in any case. The other was the calm, 'for rest' forest, where my mind felt relaxed in its nudity.

I wondered why there were no stories of little girls getting lost in forests—perhaps this was how the gendered nature of reading first became conscious to me. Satya notices women moving through the forest but doesn't know what to make of them—'Now, I suddenly remembered the old woman—she was a symbol of the civilization of the forest: for generations, her ancestors have been living in the forest... I was ready to sacrifice up to a year of my salary to find out what the old woman might have been thinking of.' I've since wondered whether the tale of the girl in the forest might have brought its reposefulness as a character in them just as suspense had trodden along with a young boy's seeking of mischief. The woman *in* the forest is quite easily turned into the woman *of* the forest, and as hunters tame the forest's wildness by maiming and killing its animals, so must men domesticate the forest woman with their irrational desire. The woman of the forest is a figure so enchanting and so imbued with mystery and eroticism that when it invades the urban imagination, it becomes the equivalent of a tiger to the hunter's imagination—the woman must be tamed.

WILD MEN AND LOST GIRLS

In *Aranyer din Ratri* (Days and Nights in the Forest), a film based on a Sunil Gangopadhyay novella, Satyajit Ray did almost the unthinkable by casting the England-bred Hindi film heroine Simi Garewal in the role of the tribal woman Duli who becomes the repository of collective lust of three young men from Calcutta who have come to the forest on a weekend break. In an adjacent forest bungalow are two sisters, one of them played with natural sophistication by Sharmila Tagore. Like strangers who find a temporary friendship in some shared commonality, these part-time bohemians seek the company of the attractive women next door. An immediate binary is set up: the cultured intelligence of the city women, set up almost as props in a memory game inside the forest, against the unnaturally coloured dark skin of the tribal woman who drinks mahua, the intoxicant, without restraint. The sexual gravitation of one of these men towards this forest woman creates an erotic tension that upsets the balance of both the social situation and the forest. There is an attempt at sexual molestation of Duli, there is the consequent outrage, and there is surface-level restoration when the men leave the forest. Two things I take from this film: the first of these is the forest bungalow that is a favourite prop that marks the Bengali's relationship with the forest like no other. The other is the effect the forest has on people of the city—an alchemy that cleanses them of conditioning and culture and offers belated employment to their latent primordiality—the jungli in the jungle, the beast of the forest. Adultery in the garden or lust in the forest—the plant world seems to turn men into amoral plants like themselves.

Aranyer din Ratri makes us aware that there is, and always must be, decorum in the forest. 'Aranya', with its own etymology, is now only for textbooks. What we have in Sanskrit colloquial are adjectives that derive from the nouns jungle, resting both meaning forest. A naughty child, for instance, is easily on, 'jungli', of the jungle, turning the human into beast in only tweak an accent. Similarly, untamed and unfamiliar flowers often have their characteristics described as 'buno', forest like. The presence of trees, for some inexplicable reason, seems to skin away the human's accrued and conditioned reserves of civility and sophistication to turn them beast-like. What is it about forests that make men reverse the social evolutionary path temporarily, to become more animal-like as it were? Is it the forest's ambivalence about hiding and revealing that abets men in becoming ancient versions of themselves?

All these questions, about time, history, evolutionary biology, suppression of desire, are condensed in the figure of the 'tribal' woman in literature about the 'liberating' effect of forest life. The forest seems to be the closest approximation of a hallucinogenic drug that allows this do-it-forget-it capsule. In this, the forest, which we now know cannot be the site of our permanent residence, is an interval, between acts of responsibility and consequence. The stag party night out before the wedding, piled with taboos and restrictions meant to be broken— that is the liberation of forest life. Not be a Roman in Rome but be a Jungli in a Jungle.

In almost direct contrast to this model of the woman nurtured by the forest is the pure and uncorrupted female character of a novel like Bankim Chandra Chattopadhyay's *Kapalkundala*. Raised by the forest as it were, Kapalkundala is untainted by human contact. While the tribal woman has distilled the forest's wildness in her, this Brahmin girl is imbued with the innocence of plants who can commit no wrong. This binary colours all such literature, and I suddenly remember an older colleague mocking my plans to visit a forest by myself. 'A woman going to the forest all alone is like a woman staying alone in a hotel.'

The figure of the woman in the forest is so romantic an idea that even in a realist narrative—reportage, to be precise—such as Yossi Ghinsberg's book, *Lost in the Jungle*, an account of the time a young

...ot lost i... ...e Bolivian rainforests in 1981 with a group of ...gers fro... ...ifferent cultures and nationalities, a girl appears ...our. Gh... ...berg fell down a waterfall and was completely alone ...lost, surv... ...ng on bare forest food, fighting animals, but more than ...nything e..., just keeping faith in his feet when he couldn't walk any more. A... then a 'miracle' happened, he says in an interview about the book, 'for two days I had the company of a girl. She appeared next to me. It was no less of a miracle if it was my imagination which had summoned her up, because it happened at the very moment I had broken down and given up.' Ghinsberg's lesson from the forest has been a simple one. 'I became a very simple person. The simple things are the most precious to me. I don't ascribe much significance to the things I have now. That feeling of touching death has never left me.'

❧

That the forest has the power to change men into trees becomes apparent to Satya as he moves through the forest interacting with its inhabitants. 'It was as though something of Jaipal's influence and something of the surrounding nature, which was so free and unfettered, was transforming me into as detached, unruffled and remote a creature as Jaipal Kumar.' This is not just forest bathing, it is eating soil like an earthworm so that the earthworm also becomes the earth. What exactly is this beauty of the forest? 'It is better for those who have to live within the strictures of domesticity never to catch sight of this beauty... Beauty that makes one mad—I'm not exaggerating even one bit; such fierce beauty is not for the faint-hearted.' Once I thought of this beauty as the absence of a gardener, akin to the photogenic beauty of untended children or the wisdom of those educated by life and not in schools. I realized, like Satya, that this had partly to do with the unexpected, with uncertainty, with fear: 'Fear sharpened the edges of the beauty around me.' That perhaps is the source of the forest's beauty—the lack of superintendence, and with it the associated freedom that such surroundings bring, the kind one feels in proximity with water and fields stretching to the horizon, the beauty of being temporarily abandoned. It is a mix of sweetness and the sublime, the beauty of a thumri, to use Satya's metaphor, mixed with fierceness, 'peace of an unbroken quiet' with an overwhelming immensity, but most of all, it is the beauty of 'no sign of a human being'.

Like all of us who get inside a forest, Satya is an autodidact, and so he is quick to give himself an education. It is not just the 'simplicity' of life in the forest—I doubt the thought occurred to the forest dwellers that their life was simple in any way—but the turning of mobility into a way of life that makes the forest such an interesting dwelling place to me. In wayward contrast to the fixed stations of trees is the movement of its dwellers inside it, a life that overturns the idea that one must return, at day end, to the place from where one began one's day. One can begin at one place at daybreak and end in another at day end, and yet one could think of this as a return home. To live in a forest is therefore to get lost in a forest, voluntarily and without regret.

How the city and its citizens have come to be considered as wiser than the forest and its residents is a subject that would one day, I am certain, be held up as a moral lesson on extinction, but there is something that bothers me elsewhere—has the forest ever been an equal place? In order to think through this naive and uneducated query, I've needed to stop and ask myself this at every bend—how is the visible militancy of the Maoists, this inevitably a reaction to state-sponsored suppression and butchery of forest life and forest dwellers, a product related to a supposed militant ethic of the forest? In this I've tried to look beyond zoocentrism, beyond a point of view of humans and animals, nation and state, to see if there is something about plant life in the forest that engenders such a political philosophy. Michael Marder, a plant philosopher, talks about a vegetal politics, a 'vegetal democracy'. This is Marder in an interview with the *Los Angeles Review of Books*:

> My question, in turn, is: 'What if we think about ourselves as political plants?' The main difference between plants and animals is that the former are not organismic units, that is to say, self-enclosed living totalities where each part is subordinated to the demands of a coherent whole. So, if we want to escape

from proto-fascism in our political thought, whereby the state is equated to an organic whole and individuals to its rather insignificant organs, we must turn toward a vegetal model of the political. The outcome of this exercise is going to be a sort of anarchic proliferation of multiplicities, of branches and twigs that retain their semi-independence while participating in the overall growth of plant-society. Such bio-politics would be incompatible with the spirit of sacrifice, logically expected within confines of an organismic arrangement; instead, it would encourage the flourishing of all within a mutually supportive environment, where there isn't a conflict—nor even a clear-cut division—between the individual and the collective. That, for me, is the most important political lesson of plants.

The refusal of individual trees to see themselves as only a part of a forest is analogical to the indifference of the forest dwellers, both in *Aranyak* and the forests of eastern India, to see themselves as part of a nation, Bharatvarsha. Trees in a forest do not know abandonment or fleeing the sinking ship. If illness—disease—comes to a neighbour, they cannot—and do not—run away or escape. Contagion is not a thing to be scared of. The 'anarchic proliferation of multiplicities, of branches and twigs that retain their semi-independence', a political system that is 'incompatible with the spirit of sacrifice' expected of citizens in a nation state is, in my mind, the spirit that the forest fosters in its members, both in the lives of plants and animals. Matthew Hall, in his book *Plants as Persons*, makes an important point behind the marginalization of plant life in our consciousness—it is their lack of violence. The lack of rebelliousness, of protest, by plant life, like the lack of resistance by forest dwellers to intrusive political systems, have left both marginalized for centuries. If plants had agency, if they could move, raise flags, cause bloodshed in humans, and if humans had not suffered from plant blindness for centuries, an ailment where we see and do not see plants because, like the sky, they are there and yet not there, they would not be treated the way they have been. If trees operated on the eye-for-an-eye ethic, for every felled tree there would be a human corpse. Imagine trees as landlords—would it be easy to uproot them?

Sumana Roy

Marder asks us to imagine plants as feudal lords. 'Ethical problems arise when we associate embeddedness in a locale with passivity. In this instance, plants appear to be our feudal serfs, completely enchained to the context of their growth, while the serfs themselves must have been treated by their feudal masters, more or less, as the crops they cultivated. The praise of dislocation and uprooting is the other side of the same coin that links mobility to active subjectivity and anchoring in a place to the passive existence of a "subjectless mass".'

⚘

Loneliness has its own networks of cure. Its closest ally, even by-product, is meditation. As one reads about Satya, telling us in first person about how the forest turns the direction of his investigation towards himself and the minutiae that constitute his life, we begin to get the sense of why sages set up forest hermitages for themselves. 'It was only here, in these lonely forests, that one had the opportunity to meditate on and be amazed by every little thing; it was the ambience which drew out such fine sensations.'

I paused to ask myself—what exactly is a forest? After all, it is only a collective noun, and I'd, for years, been scared of and apathetic to the collective noun. Was the difference between a tree and a forest similar to the difference between man and parliament or government? And more importantly, did it matter to the tree that it was in a forest, surrounded by relative trees, just as it did to a solitary individual in relation to society? French philosopher Michel Serres writes about the hegemony of the unit in his book, *Genesis*.

> Unity dazzles on at least two counts: by its sum and by its division. That herd must be singular in its totality and it must also be made up of a given number of sheep or buffalo. We want a principle, a system, an integration, and we want elements, atoms, numbers. We want them, and we make them... The irreducibly individual recedes like the horizon... We lose the particular; we've lost the world.

Serres is not talking about the tree-for-the-woods here at all. The psychological conditioning that makes us group things into collectives might make us seek comfort in a forest, but the forest tests Serres's notion of singularity too. How many trees does it take to constitute a forest? I do not mean statistics but something else, not a cheque but a cheque book.

I think men go to the forest because it is readymade. I think men go to the forest because a tree might have a birthday but a forest doesn't. I think men go to the forest because of all things man knows, only a forest is not haunted by the annual calendar. I think men go to the forest because of the uselessness of money in the jungle. I think men go to the forest to unhouse a part of what they think constitutes their permanent self. The changing nature and impermanence of the forest versus the permanence of architecture, of civilization, I found even in such expressions as 'I'll write it in her name...' Trees did not bequeath their 'property' to their progeny like that. It was up to the child to make its own life, mark its territoriality. And 'laws', the nature of legality, its human system of justice, began to seem 'unnatural' and farcical to me. There really could—should—not be a system of inheritance that ran like that. That perhaps has been the greatest lesson I have learnt from the forest—the impropriety of material inheritance.

I had been inside a forest for days, rereading *Aranyak*, living with trees and trying to adjust my body clock to theirs. It took me a long time to realize that my body had been developing its own vocabulary here. The body is terribly diffident. And the mind too conformist. I felt an intuitive sense of the forest challenging that. Middle-class morality is a universe without consequence for plant life. Here one must mention the inherent masculinity of the forest space. I cannot remember now which poet it was who called the tall spires of the trees in the forest phallic. I had no intention to be Thoreau, but from this secluded cliff I caught sounds that resembled human words in the languages I knew. Just when I felt the urge to investigate their contexts and origins, they disappeared. Sometimes it seemed to me, as I sat watching dried leaves fall from trees, that just as the written had come to be privileged over the oral, so the city over the forest.

Homesickness wouldn't be the right word for what I felt, but I missed the journeys that carried me home. At such moments, I often found myself thinking about the journey that had got me to the forest—my family having come to 'drop' me in the hope that I'd change my mind about the duration of the stay. Bablu, our driver on this trip, had told us, for no express purpose, that he was an orphan. My mother whispered, for everyone's benefit, that he looked like one. If you'd asked her what the characteristics of such a 'look' were, she would have used an invincible train of logic—I'm a mother, I know. None of us had shown any interest in her deduction. Once inside the forest, however, in a region of shorter trees compared to the giants we'd just left behind, my mother's words came to me. Weren't these trees, planted as an affirmation of the kindness of afforestation, orphans as well?

In a country with a history of gruesome violence against women, they were worried about my safety. At first I joked with them—which was better, being eaten by a tiger or being killed by a man? No one laughed at my jokes. Perhaps they had still not recovered from the shock of finding this timid woman venturing into a jungle. Their old questions came to me without answers. This, too, was an education by the forest, this break in conditioning for a dialogic nature of the world, of questions and answers. Who is safe inside a forest? Or what was history inside a forest? What is truth to a tree? Or dishonesty? For, being inside a forest is to have the sense of living in a permanent carpe diem—I felt like a tree who had been relieved of the duty of guarding and defending a future. I could not overcome my self-consciousness, to keep my desire to change into a tree in rein. Rain poured over me and the trees and I was curious to see if the rain, the headless rain, wet us in the same manner. Looking at old trees, I suffered from anxiety. Did they suffer from dementia? The detachment, even the indifference, that the upper part of the tree showed for the lower parts, where once there were young stems, left me uncomfortable. Had they forgotten their childhood, their youth?

The Forest Ranger came to visit me once. One is always an exile inside a forest, and so is vanvas, he joked. His words about the near arbitrary cluster choice of trees in one space turned the forest into an 'achievement' of human civilization. When I asked him about the history of this forest, he had none except the post-independence life of this territory that now houses trees. Why are there no histories of our forests except in statistical data about narratives of growth and loss? Why doesn't the history of a nation include the history of its forests?

Sometimes animals taken out of their natural habitats such as these forests go mad, the officer told me, as if passing a piece of information that would be important to me some day.

'And the trees?' I asked about them, those living beings without 'brains'.

The officer was keen to show me the bureaucratic life of trees in a reserved forest as something almost akin to our modern life in a nation state. My mind wandered away from the queue of his forest department terminology. I grew impatient to ask him whether plants were given character and transfer and migration certificates when they were moved from this reserved forest to a park in the city or another such forest.

But he wouldn't stop. Having just learnt about my training in literature, he began reciting four-line rhymes that had been created and curated by the forest department over many decades. Apart from an ostentatious and moralistic love for plant life, there was little to recommend them. When I laughed after one such rhyme, he thought it was an appreciation, but I was actually being tickled by a ridiculous thought: imagine a literary festival where poets read out their poems to a packed audience inside a forest. Only, instead of people, the audience consists of trees standing, as always, in attention mode.

Once he'd finished praising himself and the forest department, I asked him why forest ashrams, once a staple of schooling, had not been part of the department's initiatives. He smiled, but gave no answer. Later, as we were about to leave, in a voice much lower than the one he'd used so far, he said, 'My father's uncle studied in one such school in Bangladesh. Of course it wasn't Bangladesh then. He told my father—I never saw the man; he died before I was born—that it wasn't actually their guru, trained in Sanskrit and mathematics, from whom they learnt the most. The trees were the real teachers in that forest ashram.'

I suddenly had the feeling of the man being my relative. The trees in the forest were Ekalavyas. They had all sacrificed an important part of themselves for men who would not acknowledge them.

On what must be the forest's northern margin, I noticed a farmer working on the field. He was coaxing two things at the same time—his cows and the soil. His plea was for both to move. Suddenly he and his props turned into an antonym of the adjoining forest for me. The visibility of the human agency, its need for a system of barter with the plant world, and perhaps more than everything else, this expectation of the plant world as a readymade kitchen—all these are a contrast to the forest and its crisp freedom. It is this opposition, between the exhibition of human control in agricultural toil and the complete invisibility of offices and work chambers inside the forest that has made it so attractive to weekday-imprisoned office employees. And it is this sound of the breaking and unshackling of chains that results in the noise of excursions in the forest.

And yet, in spite of the proto-revolutionary spirit of the forest, there are no celebrities in the plant world. In this I had already arrived as a plant, fame and its technology never having mattered to me. In fact, I have to confess that I laughed at expressions like 'world famous'—the Forest Ranger had used it for a species of tree found in the forest.

There was something else I learnt from trees during my stay in the forest—it was about the nature of mistakes. All winter, the previous year, I had worn layers of protective woollen clothing to shield myself from the cold. I'd suffered from pneumonitis, the previous year and it was my ambition to lead an antibiotic free winter.

I failed.

When I searched for that one weakness that had allowed the virus in, it took me days to track it down: a five-minute conversation in the open with a friend on a late winter evening. It annoyed me, this nature of life—a murderer's good deeds obliterated against one wrong act. The cold got into me in spite of the tight carefulness of my regime on all the days except that one. This was the thing about plants—they did not know the aberrational life. There was no exception to the rule in their universe. Routine was not boredom for them. Difference, of the 'let's do something different' or 'out of the box' kind, was alien to their system. The freight of doubt and the weight of hope did not affect plants. That is also why I had wanted to be like them.

There was something else too: there is no concept of hygiene in the plant world, particularly in a forest. And there is no distinction between dirt and cleanliness in this plant commune.

And yet, in spite of how much the forest gives, how easily it lets one become a temporary plant or tree, we kill the forest. We kill those we love most. To know the Buddha, kill the Buddha. And so, in spite of what and how much Satya gets from the forest, how he becomes the forest as it were, he has to destroy it. 'Yet, I grieved, knowing that the forests of Narhabaihar would not stand for long. I loved the place so greatly, but my own hands had destroyed it. In two years the entire estate would be settled and would be taken over by ugly tolas and dirty hutments. It had taken hundreds of years of fervent meditation, of sadhana, to create Narhabaihar; nature had fashioned it lovingly with her own hands. The exquisite forests and the distant winding open spaces would be completely erased.'

The obverse of Satya is two of my favourite forest men, one from literature, another from outside it. There is Jean Giono's famous story, 'The Man Who Planted Trees', from the middle of the twentieth century. Written in the first person, in French, the narration begins forty years ago, when the narrator 'was taking a long trip on foot over mountain heights...in that ancient region where the Alps thrust down into Provence'. This is barren land, and 'nothing grew there but wild lavender'. Thirsty, he looks for water from a spring or well near a cluster of houses nearby, but it is all dry, and people have fled or abandoned their houses a long time ago. Walking for five hours, and still without water, he chances upon a 'small black silhouette' and mistakes it for a solitary tree. Getting closer, he finds the figure to be a shepherd who

Sumana Roy

gives him with a drink of water.

The shepherd exhibits the traits of a solitary life—he hardly speaks, he lives a tidy life amidst abandoned houses which once belonged to families engaged in colliery and mining. There was nothing extraordinary about him except his after-dinner activity: 'The shepherd went to fetch a small sack and poured out a heap of acorns on the table. He began to inspect them, one by one, with great concentration, separating the good from the bad... When he had set aside a large enough pile of good acorns he counted them out by tens, meanwhile eliminating the small ones or those which were slightly cracked... When he had thus selected one hundred perfect acorns he stopped and we went to bed.'

The shepherd gave him easy permission to both rest in his humble cottage and to accompany him during his rounds of shepherding. The narrator noticed that the shepherd carried an iron rod with him. After the sheep had spread out to graze, 'he began thrusting his iron rod into the earth, making a hole in which he planted an acorn; then he refilled the hole. He was planting oak trees. I asked him if the land belonged to him. He answered no... He was not interested in finding out whose it was. He planted his acorns with the greatest care'. The shepherd had planted one hundred thousand acorns over the last three years—only twenty thousand had sprouted. He expected only a half of this to survive—even then, there would be ten thousand oak trees in the region.

The name of this man was Elzéard Bouffier—once the owner of a farm in the lowlands, he had lost his wife and son and retreated into the solitude of these lands which he came to love and pity, for he felt them dying from lack of vegetation and trees large enough to hold the soil together. In 1915, after the war, when the narrator returned to the place, he was surprised to find Elzéard alive. The oaks, now more than ten thousand in number, had changed the place. They had changed Elzéard's livelihood too—he was no longer a shepherd but a beekeeper. The sheep had been eating up his new plants; the bees, on the other hand, indulged the growth of the trees through their habits of pollination. 'Creation seemed to come about in a sort of chain reaction. He did not worry about it; he was determinedly pursuing his task in all its simplicity; but as we went back toward the village I saw water flowing in brooks that had been dry since the memory of man.'

In time, people, and particularly the bureaucracy, began to grow curious about how this 'natural' forest had suddenly come to be. Forest officers began visiting the place, offering recommendations and prescribing restrictions to Elzéard, but the man continued doing what he did. No one knew—or would even believe—that it was possible for a man to singlehandedly plant a forest. When the narrator last meets Elzéard in 1945, two years before his death, he is stunned to see how a desert had been turned into a green economy, with agriculture, bus services, hamlets and villages, and of course the forest, now home to men, animals, birds, and new secrets of water.

Jean Giono's story is a fable, yes, but there is such honesty in the narrative that like me, many readers had mistaken this to be a report of a true life. I was inspired, when I first read it, to replicate the model in barren surroundings. I found that I was not alone in this—a fruit seller once told me that he dumped rotten fruits by roadsides in the hope that a few of those would grow into trees. He even gave me the location and address of mango and jackfruit trees that he had 'planted' in this manner. It was true, there was an Elzéard inside all of us—a man who was capable of planting a forest. And yet, when I encountered the story of Jadav Payeng, I was incredulous.

Payeng is Elzéard in real life, and in one of those mysterious and even incredible ways that life imitates art, Jadav Payeng, without any knowledge of Giono's fable, had created a forest all by himself. Born in Assam, exactly a decade after *The Man Who Planted Trees* became available to the English speaking world, Jadav Payeng was only sixteen when he noticed dead reptiles on the sandbars of the Brahmaputra River. He realized that this was due to the absence of any tree cover in the region, but the bureaucracy remained indifferent until the Assam Forestry officials adopted two hundred hectares of land to plant bamboo. Jadav found employment in the project for five years, but unlike the rest who left after the completion of the project, he has continued planting, for the last thirty-two years, trees in Aruna

Sumana Roy

Chapori, now a 550 hectare forest in what was once a barren sandbar. Awards and recognition began coming to him after 2008, when a herd of elephants found shelter in 'his' forest after destroying settlements in the neighbourhood—the Padma Shri, the country's fourth highest civilian honour, came to him recently, but perhaps the most endearing recognition for the 'Forest Man of India' has been having the forest named after him, 'Mulai Kathoni Bari', Mulai being his nickname.

The parallels between Elzéard and Jadav's self-sufficient technology are astounding. In an interview with Ananya Borgohain, he says, 'This reserve is as long as the stretch from Paris to Switzerland. But it has no maintenance problem as such because it is comfortably grown on country wisdom and practical applications rather than any scientific measures. I don't have staffers. I had started by building a bamboo platform on the top of each sapling I planted and covered them with earthen pots with holes in them. The water would leak on the plants below and water them that way. I also used termites, ants, earthworms and similar insects to enhance the fertility of the soil.' His success has been to turn a garden into a forest, a system capable of nurturing itself.

That is why my favourite character in *Aranyak* is not Satya but Jugalprasad, who is obsessed with collecting unfamiliar plants and planting them in new spaces. The forest is a Hermes-like figure, moving between states, a figure of transitions and translations. Planting trees is the only way to kill death, to achieve immortality, a fact Jugalprasad recognizes. Jugalprasad is that 'madman', and also that oxymoron, a farmer of the forest. The more I read about him, the more I identified with him—he was the kind of person I'd wanted to be. When a character in the novel says that Jugalprasad is irresponsible in that he doesn't look after his family, but 'just wanders around in the forest', I wonder whether there is a word that could hold in it the temperament and ambition that characterizes a flâneur in the forest. 'The man was spending his own time and money in order to beautify huge areas of forestland where he had no claim over any piece of land. All this work, with no selfish motive,' reports Satya. A man whose only ambition had been to spot unfamiliar plant life and introduce it to the forests in Lobtulia, he might now be considered an ecologist's nightmare—

'foreign' plants have often upset the nitrogen balance of the soil. But it is impossible to not be emotionally swayed by Jugalprasad's dedication and be moved by his devotion to the religion of the forest: 'I wished only to introduce these flowers and creepers and trees which were unknown to any one place. I've been doing this all my life. I have not grown old in the task.'

For every Jugalprasad there is a Satya, for every forest the root of a tree that has lost its home. 'Perhaps a time would come when men would no more be able to see forests: all they would see would be fields of crops, or the chimneys of jute and cotton mills. They would come then to this secluded forestland, as though on a pilgrimage. For these people, yet to come, let the forest stay pristine, undisturbed,' says Satya, in a moment of prescience, after clearing the forest for human settlement. That is the hyphenated truth about the forests that remain. When I was a child, I encountered two phrases constantly—'The King of the Forest', about an animal, 'Vanaspati', the King of Trees, about a tree. Living in the forest and reading about Satya's destruction of its plant life had led to the extinction of that utopia. Man was the new Vanaspati.

Subhash Mukhopadhyay, a Bangla poet now remembered mostly for his Marxist poetry, wrote a poem about Rama's journey to the forest, his vanvas. The axis around which the poem turns is the opposition between Rama and his father Dasharath, how it ought to have been the father who should have gone to the forest for his vanaprastha, and the unnaturalness of a young man, a future king, spending his time in the forest. This poem, which had been a favourite in my early adulthood, came to me as I walked out of the forest after my long and solitary stay. His time in the forest had changed Rama's life and career. Could my time there have changed me?

Is the person who goes inside a forest the same as the one coming out of it?

Part VIII

Under the Greenwood Tree
—William Shakespeare, *As You Like It*

SITTING UNDER A TREE

Having never asked for a birthday gift in my life, I found it difficult to do, especially when I was asking it of a man who has never cared for the aura around birthdays.

'I'd like to turn forty under *that* tree,' I said.

Like most women, I'd have liked to believe that a husband of long years would be able to interpret the italicized word in my voice. Like most men, my husband looked askance at me, trying hard to recover any clues he might have missed from a previous conversation.

We were talking in our bedroom, the room in which I spend most of my time when I am at home. It is an unusually large room. In one corner, by the giant windows that I open to let in the cool northern air, stands a big tree. I use the word 'big' consciously—it is tall, much taller than my husband who is six feet tall. But it was dead. I had found it abandoned by the roadside near a church and had felt an onrush of affection and attraction for it immediately, of the kind that it is possible to feel only for dead plant life, not dead animals, or dead men. Soon after, the tree had become an occupant in our bedroom, the carpenter having given it wooden stilts so that death had not been able to take away what it immediately does—the dignity of the vertical position. Beneath that leafless tree now sat a statue of the Buddha, his eyes closed.

My husband turned to the tree and then to me. He looked confused. If his wife wanted to meet her fortieth year by sitting under that tree, who was he to refuse? Especially as, given the kind of person he is, he wouldn't have been able to remember how his wife had brought in her thirtieth or the thirty-ninth—sitting on a chair or crouched under a table.

'Sure,' he replied after some thought. He sounded quite happy. 'I' wanted to sit under that tree, I had not asked that of him. Not yet that is.

'Will you take me to meet the Bodhi tree then?' I asked.

I was aware of the circuit that would break inside the travel-shy man. It was one thing to buy a young plant from the nursery and make an acquaintance with the stranger, quite another to travel more than 600 kilometres to meet an old tree. I heard out his silence with a mixture of amusement and annoyance.

'Sure,' he said again, in the tone of one convincing himself.

'Why not a forest?' he asked later at night.

'That's like comparing apples to oranges,' I replied, annoyed. Couldn't he see the difference between a solitary tree and a forest?

But after he'd fallen asleep, I wondered why I'd been so annoyed. When the answer came to me I had to resist the urge to shake him out of his sleep. When he turned restlessly in his sleep I said to him, 'One goes to a forest to get lost. One goes to the Bodhi tree to find oneself.'

Half asleep, he replied: 'In both something is missing.'

I remember not sleeping that night and feeling terribly alone, the kind of loneliness that is stoked by the night. I remember thinking that all the world loves an infant. But as we age, the number of lovers we have dwindle. Our journey towards death, punctuated by birthdays, is a preparation for solitude. It suddenly struck me that my husband's query, about choosing a solitary tree over a forest, could compare with that journey, our lovers reduced to no one but the self. Looked at another way, this was my humble, homemade interpretation of Buddhism, in which the focus is only on the self, for the world is beyond our control. And so a tree, not a forest.

❧

In all this contemplation of sitting or standing under trees, a few things come to mind. I grew up in a locality that was bordered by Aamtala and Pakurtala on either side, the first a neighbourhood whose name literally meant 'under a mango tree', the second a crossroad that meant roughly the same, except that instead of the mango, it was the pakur, the portia tree. 'Tala', meaning under, was a common suffix to the names of trees, and these had been used for naming hamlets, neighbourhoods, even towns and villages. In them is the whiff of an older history, of a world, in which trees and their ecology of shade were important.

'Nothing happens' under a tree, and yet something does, something must, something so subtle that our eyes fail to register the changes. In a poem titled 'Gachhtawla', Under a Tree, the Bengali poet Sunil Ganguly recounts the history of religion and the history of hate, of Rama and Rabindranath, of churches and gurdwaras, and the skies over Bangladesh's Chittagong and Bengal's Bankura and their indifference to borders of nations and their fairy-tale borders. He calls out to Kanai and Kamal, two young men from the Hindu and Muslim communities, and asks them to join him in watching the procession of human history driven by the madness of 'old fools'. 'And we laugh at them from under a tree,' he says. And suddenly the polarity of two worlds floats to the surface with that line—the foolish violence of action-filled human history counterpoised against the 'nothing happens' world beneath the tree.

Poets have always seemed to find something under a tree. D. H. Lawrence finds a similar counterpoint to modern history's frenetic march:

Under the almond tree, the happy lands
Provence, Japan, and Italy repose,
And passing feet are chatter and clapping of those
Who play around us, country girls clapping their hands.

The poem is titled 'Letter from Town: The Almond Tree', and in it we find busy civilizations resting under a tree—'Provence, Japan, and Italy repose', after the labour of these countries in the studio and the battlefield. Lawrence is unambiguous about the harvest of such an experience—under a tree are 'the happy lands'. Around it is movement, of feet and hands, of young and the old, but under it is rest, the rest of temporary and happy forgetfulness.

It is this that Shakespeare memorialized in the play *As You Like*

It—my childhood memories are annotated by these lines in my father's baritone, he who had been raised in the shade of trees in his tiny village on the Indo-Bangladesh border:

Under the greenwood tree
Who loves to lie with me,
And turn his merry note
Unto the sweet bird's throat,
Come hither, come hither, come hither:
    Here shall he see
    No enemy
But winter and rough weather.

Who doth ambition shun
And loves to live i' the sun,
Seeking the food he eats,
And pleased with what he gets,
Come hither, come hither, come hither:
    Here shall he see
    No enemy
But winter and rough weather.

This immediate abandonment of worldly ambition would be familiar to anyone who has stood under a tree. Being under a tree is a holiday from reason—who has seen a bureaucrat clearing files under a tree after all? Imagine the Buddha with a briefcase, sitting under a tree. The shunning of ambition, time without structure, a carriage without rivals or enemies, not to mention the barter economy of oxygen and carbon dioxide that keeps animals alive—all these are gifts from life under a tree.

THE BUDDHA AND THE BODHI TREE

The Bodhi tree is a fig tree, also known as the peepul, *Ficus religiosa*. When I told him about my trip to Bodh Gaya, a colleague who is a professor of Sanskrit said he hoped I would not forget the rich religious history of the peepul before the Buddha. I wasn't particularly interested in what he had to say but he seemed terribly passionate about the subject and wanted me to know that John Marshall, the archaeologist who had discovered the Harappa and Indus Valley ruins, wrote about the peepul being worshipped in Mohenjodaro. My colleague did not use the words 'fig' or 'peepul'—his word for the tree was 'Asvathha', literally meaning 'horses' stand' in Pali; it was now a Bangla word. The root of the peepul was associated with the Brahman, the Supreme Being, he said. And then the stories: Yama, the god of death, spent time under this tree, as also the 'gods of the Thirty-Third Heaven'; 'the Soma-vessel and the sacred fire-drill are made out of this Tree'. His source for this knowledge was Dipak Kumar Barua's *The Bodhi Tree and Mahabodhi Mahavihara Temple at Buddha Gaya*. When he shared his copy of the book with me, I began to read greedily.

Barua spends great energy on collecting linguistic gossip and minutiae about the tree, the fig tree's names in various languages, their etymologies and the contexts that might have birthed them. He also describes the tree as a botanical specimen—'generally epiphytic', the upper surface of the leaf is shiny 'and the lower side is minutely tuberculated when it is dry'; 'the shape of the leaf is ovate-rotund, and narrowed upwards'; it produces dark berries; 'the tree grows to a height of about 100 feet, and the leaves suspended on their long flexible petioles rustle in the slightest breeze'. To the leaves, Barua gives a spiritual dimension: he quotes from L. A. De Silva's books on beliefs and practices in Buddhism to make his point. 'It is believed that the mysterious quivering and rustling of the leaves of this tree are supposed to be stirrings of a divine afflatus and the whisperings of divine or supernatural communications.'

On the train, first from New Jalpaiguri to Patna, and then from Patna to Gaya, I prepared my husband for our meeting with the Bodhi tree with stories that I had collected from various sources, including scripture and popular lore. The latter I found more interesting—'impurity' is always a delicious ingredient.

Gautama was twenty-nine—exactly a decade younger than I was then—when he abandoned everything, family, kingdom, comfort, and much else, in a quest for truth. Disillusioned by human suffering, and curious about its cause (so that he could find a way to eliminate it), Gautama kept walking until he found a place where he could think.

Gautama stopped in the village of Uruvela, now about six miles from the train station in Gaya. The moment of arrival, 'rest' and the rest, are recorded in various ways in the Buddhist scriptures. Here it is in Dipak Kumar Barua's narration: 'The Bodhi Tree of the present Buddha, that is, Gotama Buddha, was said to have sprung on the day He was born and so it was referred to as the Sahajata. As a Bodhisatta or Bodhisattva who was striving for the attainment of Buddhahood, Gotama passed a day in the grove of Sala trees at Uruvela and at the evening walked along the wide road, towards the Bodhi Tree accompanied by divinities. Under it He sat down cross-legged with a firm resolution: "Skin, sinew, and bone may dry up as it will, my body, but without attaining Complete Enlightenment, I will not leave this 'seat', so resolved the great Bodhisattva as He sat under the sacred Bodhi Tree, Asvattha, hallowed down the ages."'

The *Vinaya Pitaka* tells us that the Buddha spent a week looking at the tree in gratitude, and subsequently gave permission to his devotees to worship it. This piece of information I gathered from the Maha Bodhi Vandana, a Buddhist prayer:

I bow down my head and salute the King Bodhi Tree which was worshipped for seven days by the Buddha with his tears, I bow

to the King of Trees, sitting at the root of which the Buddha
defeated Mara and eventually discovered the Four Noble Truths,
I worship the Mahabodhi tree that was worshipped by the
Buddha.

The Bodhi tree, however, is not the only tree that is worshipped in
Bodh Gaya, as the catalogue of trees from this Buddhist prayer in
Benimadhab Barua's translation reveals: 'I make my adoration firstly to
the place of Enlightenment, secondly to the place of Animesalocana,
thirdly to the Cankamana...', and then it comes to the names of the
other trees—the Ajapalanyagrodha-mula-Chaitya, the 'shrine under
the neat herded Banyan', the Muchalinda-mula-Chaitya, the 'shrine
under the Muchalinda Tree', and the Rajayatana Chaitya, the shrine
under the Rajayatana Tree.

It did not take long for my husband to guess what I was getting
at, behind the scaffolding of quotations from the Buddhist Jataka tales
and scriptures. 'Why worship the tree and not an image, an idol or a
relic?' Why did the Buddha allow a tree to be a convenient substitute
for himself?

The *Kalingabodhi Jataka* tells us about the disappointment of the
people of Sravasti at not being able to meet the Buddha who would
often be away on his travels through the subcontinent. Anathapindika,
the merchant celebrated for his large-heartedness in these tales, made a
request to Ananda, Gautama's cousin, and also one of his first disciples:
'When the Blessed One is not present in the Jetavana Vihara, it appears
to be empty and the people do not have any object to worship.
Kindly ask Tathagata whether it is possible to make any permanent
arrangement for worshipping Him continuously during His absence
throughout the day'. At the time it was common to worship one of the
three—'shrine of a relic of the body', 'shrine of a relic of a memorial',
'shrine of relic of use or wear'. The Buddha rejected all these options;
he asked Ananda to bring a seed of Uruvela's Bodhi tree and plant it
in the surroundings of the Jetavana monastery. This was done, and like
it is possible in only such miracles, when Ananthapindika planted the
seed, it turned into a plant almost immediately, and then into a tree,
like it is possible only in miracles. The King of Kosala had the tree

surrounded by eight hundred gold and silver jars in which bloomed eight hundred blue lotuses in sweet-smelling water. This tree survives as the 'Ananda Bodhi' in history—it can be seen near the ruins of Sravasti's Gandhakuti. The *Kalingabodhi Jataka* makes the equivalence between the Buddha and the Bodhi tree clear: 'the tree itself was regarded as the living symbol of the Master's presence'.

The story of the travel of a branch of the Mahabodhi Tree to Sri Lanka is quite similar. The *Samantapasadika* brings to us today what reads like a history of violence unleashed on the Bodhi tree during its travel from Uruvela to Sri Lanka. What is inescapable in this narration is the role of Emperor Ashoka. Here is Dipak Kumar Barua's translation of the narration from *Mahavamsa*: 'The King Dharmasoka insisted on cutting the Bodhi Tree with his own hands at the Bodhimanda, he himself placed it on the ship that was to take it down the Ganga, and he accompanied it as far as the place of embarkation at Tamralipti. He shed copious tears on parting with it, and confined it to the care of his daughter Sanghamitra, who was going to Sinhala with eleven nuns; for though Mahindra could ordain priests, the Law only permitted a woman to ordain priestesses or nuns.'

Vamsa literature mythicizes the Sri Lankan Bo tree, its travels, its planting and taking root in such a way that disbelief becomes unimportant to our sensibility. Instead, I am led to wonder about a culture thousands of years ago, one that could place a tree at the core of its belief system when there was no threat of the environmental apocalypse that generates so much of our tree love today. I quote again from Barua for the man's literal and unfiltered translation brings so much of the awe around the tree alive, this in spite of his acute awareness of Mahanama relating 'all these miracles... without the slightest hesitation or criticism'.

> The Tree was carried by sixteen persons of sixteen different castes, who deposited it in a magnificent Hall prepared for it. He (King Devanampiya Tissa) invested the sacred branch with the sovereignty of Lanka, and himself for three days and three nights, stood as sentinel at the door of the Hall offering it rich presents... At sunrise, it was carried in by the northern gate of

the city, through which it was borne in procession, and it was taken out by the southern gate to be conveyed to the beautiful garden of Mahamegha, where it was planted. Sixteen princes clad in the most brilliant garments stood ready to receive it; but the Branch, breaking loose from the hands of men, suddenly rose in the air, where it remained before the astonished gaze of the crowd, lighted up by a halo of six luminous rays. It came down again at sunset, and planted itself in the soil, and for seven days a protecting cloud shaded it and watered it with salutary rain. Fruit grew on it in an instant, and the King was able to propagate throughout the Island the marvellous Tree, the Bodhi, the promise of eternal salvation.

One must remember that all this takes place more than two hundred years after the death of the Buddha, and for a tree to retain that kind of an aura needed an uncommon communal belief. It must take more faith to believe in a tree than in an idol—the peepul tree is common in these parts of Bihar, what would make this one more special than the rest?

There is a constant connection between Gautama and plant life. In an interesting—even if a bit catalogue-like—essay titled 'Forest and Trees Associated with Lord Buddha', Basantu Bidari mentions more than sixty-one forests in Buddhist literature, primarily the *Tripitakas, Attakathas, Jatakas*. He also writes about Gautama Buddha's fondness for the 'vana' (forest abode; vana is forest): 'Lord Buddha during his travel generally spent his night either near the pond or in the Amravana (mango grove)/Amalakavanat (emblic myrobalan)/Arandyavana (natural forest)'. He then goes on to mention Jetavana, a forest belonging to Prince Jeta of Sravasti, where the Buddha 'spent twenty one of his forty five rainy seasons' teaching many of his Sutras; Nyagrodhvana in Kapilavastu, 'the place where Lord Buddha met his father Suddhodana for the first time after the enlightenment'; the Mahavanas of Vaisali, Uruvela, Kapilavastu, where the Buddha spent many monsoons; Lumbini Vana, where he was born; Venuvana in

Kajangala and Rajgriha, where King Bimbisara first met the Buddha; Amravana, which was a gift to the Buddha from a mendicant, and where his son Rahul is said to have spent a significant period of time; and the Ambapali vana, where the Buddha spent the last year of his life.

The Buddha's life is entwined with trees in other ways as well. Mayadevi, his mother, is said to have given birth to Siddhartha by holding the Ashoka tree. Bidari quotes from B. D. Kyokai's *The Teaching of Buddha*: 'All about here (Lumbini) were Ashoka blossoms and in delight she reached out her right arm to pluck a branch and as she did so a prince was born.' Enlightenment, of course, came under the peepul tree, as did the Buddha's first meal after enlightenment, in four alms bowls. He is said to have died under a tree as well, two sala trees in fact. Bidari reports, 'In this panel (now in the Indian Museum, Calcutta) Buddha is seen lying on his right side with one leg resting over the other on a couch spread between two sala trees...' There are Buddhist tales about Gautama and mango trees as well as banyan trees. Sitting under a tree seems to be inextricably linked with the Buddha's spiritual life. Bidari writes this about Gautama's first 'trance': 'While a young man living at his father's palace, he was brought to sit under a Jamun (Jambu) tree, where he was to witness a ploughing contest as representative for the king. While sitting he practiced yogic breathing and attained his first trance. When his attendants returned sometime later, they noticed that the shadows of the other trees nearby had moved, but that of the Jamun tree had remained stationary over the meditating prince'. He was also sitting under a tree when he first met his father after his Enlightenment—it was a banyan. At Yashodhara's swayamvar, Siddhartha unleashed an arrow that flew past seven tada trees and eventually disappeared. Bidari mentions a long catalogue of plants and trees that are repeatedly mentioned in literature about the Buddha—among the many familiar botanical names from the subcontinent, I am surprised to note his mention of the 'khursani', Nepali for chilli.

But this is not all. John S. Strong, in an essay entitled 'Gandhakuti: The Perfumed Chamber of the Buddha', writes about the perfumed chamber where the Buddha is said to have spent a significant part of his day: 'Buddhaghosa mentions it was to the gandhakuti that lay people used to come every afternoon to honour the Buddha with offerings of perfumes, flowers, and so on.' But this gandhakuti was no permanent residence, for his devotees built perfumed chambers for him wherever he went. One of these, for instance, was built by a gardener who, I was thrilled to note, was my namesake: 'Sumana, a gardener, meets the Blessed One and decides to offer him some of his lotus: first he threw two handfuls of flowers over the Teacher. These remain suspended like the curtain of a pavilion. The next two handfuls he threw descended on his left side and remained suspended. Thus eight measures of flowers, eight handfuls in all, surrounded the Tathagata on four sides. In front, it was as if there was a gate for him to enter.'

But such perfumed chambers were built for the Buddha even when he wasn't present. Strong tells us, with copious quotations from the *Purnavadana*, that like the Bodhi tree, the perfumed chamber of fragrant flowers came to stand in for the Buddha as well. Strong gives the example of Purna who is in Sronaparanta while the Buddha is in Sravasti. After building a gandhakuti, Purna invites the absent Buddha into the chamber, 'climbs to the top of the prasada, burns incense, and throws flowers in the direction of Sravasti where the Buddha is residing'.

Ananda, his cousin, who had once obeyed the Buddha's instruction of planting a seed from Uruvela's Bodhi tree in Sravasti so that the tree could serve as his body double as it were, is said to have treated the gandhakuti in Jetavana in a similar fashion. Arriving there after the death of the Buddha, 'and having saluted the Gandhakuti once dwelt in by Him of the Ten Powers, he opened the door, took down the chair and dusted it thoroughly, swept out the Gandhakuti, threw away the rubbish of the faded garlands, moved about the chair and the bed and then put them back in their proper places and performed all the round of duties that had to be performed in the lifetime of the Blessed One. And whilst he was performing them, at the times for sweeping out the bathroom, setting the water ready and so on, he would salute the Gandhakuti and say: "Lo, Blessed One, now is your time for washing, now is the time for expounding the Law... now is the time for lying down like a lion, and so on".'

This adoption of flowers, for fragrance and beauty as well as for their covert symbolism, marks Sukhavati, which in the *Lotus Sutra*, for instance, is described as 'pure, clean, devoid of stones, grit and gravel... strewed with flowers'. Strong calls this a 'future Buddha Land', a version of paradise, Sukhavati, the land of 'such' happiness, a counterpoint to this life on earth that, according to the Buddha, runs to a philosophy of dukkha, suffering. In the Vajrasana cell at Bodh Gaya, outside which I saw monks from Southeast Asia performing what looked like yogic postures, is an inscription that suggests that it was a gandhakuti— archaeologist Alexander Cunningham discovered the dedication of 'this lofty perfumed house which is like unto a flight of steps to heaven'. This corroborates Strong's argument of a Buddhist future land being one composed of flowers—there are no rough surfaces there, no stones, no pebbles, a smooth space swept clean all the time, and perfumed by flowers. It was this culture of an extravagant emphasis on sweet smells that I encountered at Bodh Gaya—camphor and incense, yes, but also an ostentatious offering of flowers. Beautiful and intricate bouquets with the lotus as their centrepiece were placed in front of every statue of the Buddha, monks and nuns and tourists left offerings of flowers everywhere on the premises, but most remarkable was the everyday recreation of the Buddhist legend of the blooming of blue lotuses from Gautama's footsteps, moments after he had taken a walk after his Enlightenment.

Living amidst a Hindu-dominated symbolism of the lotus had left me illiterate about the importance the Buddha had placed on this flower in his teachings. The *Satapatha Brahmana* says this about the lotus: 'The lotus means the waters, and this earth is a leaf thereof; even as the lotus leaf here spread on the waters, so this earth lies spread on the waters.' The padmasana is one way of turning into a lotus, and I found its innocence charming—it was this easy, was it, to turn into a lotus just by holding one's spine and folding one's legs? And as if that bit of self-deception wasn't enough, one could try to remain unaffected by the world, its scratchy sadness, dukkha, like the Buddha: 'Just as a lotus born and grown in the water rises to the surface and remains unsmeared by the water, even so, the Tathagata, born in the world, full grown by the world remains unaffected by the world.'

꙼

As I read through the Buddha's teachings, I began to see that all that the Buddha asked men to be, bereft of greed and desire, and everything that caused suffering, especially the vanity that makes us obsess about control, a life with these subtractions, was actually the life of a tree. The Middle Path, one that he advised as taking a median between extremes of austerity and hedonism, it seemed to me, was the Buddha's way of asking us to turn tree-like. For among all living beings, it is only plant life that is neither a glutton nor ascetic, neither greedy nor anorexic. A tree does not—cannot—survive on the polarities of extremes, and more than anything else, a tree had managed to escape the assembly line of dukkha, suffering. The Eightfold Path, with its emphasis on right view and right action and right effort and right concentration and so on, everything seemed to fit. Even 'right speech'. Wrote the poet Santideva in the *Bodhicariyavatara*: 'Trees do not speak harsh words, nor do they try to please by artifice; when shall I have the opportunity to live with those who are happy to live with the trees?'

In his book *Water in Culture*, J. B. Disanayaka writes about a teaching assembly where the Buddha held a flower in one hand and winked at his disciples. Among all of them, only Mahakasyapa understood what Gautama meant. Zen Buddhists have chosen to interpret this as an illustration of mind-to-mind communication, like that between flowers. So the 'Right Speech' in the Buddha's prescribed Eightfold Path could be, after all, wordless communication, like that between trees.

A kind and hospitable person, the Buddha said, was like a banyan tree welcoming tired travellers into its soothing shade. The *Milindapanha* is more direct in its instruction to turn into a tree: As a tree makes no distinction in the shade it gives, we ought to make no distinction between people, whether they are thieves, murderers, enemies, or oneself. The *Buddhacharita*, which gives us a detailed life of the Buddha, compares the practice of a spiritual life to a tree 'whose fibres are patience, whose flowers are virtue, whose boughs are awareness and wisdom, which is rooted in resolution and which bears the fruit of Dhamma'. Almost everywhere in Buddhist teachings I encounter the veneration of the tree—I notice that this is expressed as gratitude more for the tree's shade-giving ability rather than its fruit-producing skill. This realization directs me to what I had originally set out to find—what was so special about sitting under a tree? In this relation between the tree and its nurturing shade, the Buddhists find parables of gratitude. 'Of the tree in whose shade one sits or lies, not a branch of it should he break, for if he did he would be a betrayer of a friend, an evil doer,' Ankura teaches in the *Vimanavatthu*.

Taking note of the wood for the trees as it were, the Buddha uses the 'sameness' of all wood and its utilitarianism to make a case against casteism in the Hindu society of the time. In the *Kannakatthala Sutta*, the Buddha tells King Pasenadi that there is little to distinguish dry teak wood from dry mango wood or dry fig wood when it came to using them as firewood. In the same way there is nothing to distinguish one person from another on the basis of caste. The udumbara—the fig—tree is a favourite with most Buddhist teachers. Its hidden flowers offer themselves easily to metaphors—the Buddhist teachers turn these flowers into morals about insubstantiality. Here is an illustration from the *Sutta Nipata*: He who cannot find substance in any realm of being, like flowers which one seeks in vain from the fig tree, such a monk gives up on life here, just as a snake sheds its old skin. The futility of looking for life's core comes with examples drawn exclusively from plant life in this instruction from *Visuddhimagga*: a reed has no core, neither does a castor oil fruit, a fig flower, an asetavachcha tree, a plantain trunk, a bubble of water, and so on.

As with any object of veneration, trees too have had to deal with hatred directed towards them by those jealous of their hold on the imagination and lives of those devoted to them. In the *Kunalavadana* I learned about Emperor Ashoka's obsessive attachment to the Bodhi tree, and his show of affection by offering her his favourite jewels. This secret love, that often led Ashoka to spend nights under the Bodhi tree, away from his palace, quite naturally aroused his wife's suspicion. And so the jealous Queen Tisyarakshita, mistaking the Bo tree for a woman, a 'sapatni', a co-wife, ordered for it to be killed and destroyed. Magic, charms and chants, and a fire led to the withering of the tree. This Ashoka counteracted by bathing the tree daily with milk, and for five years, the tree was worshipped with thousands of vessels of milk and scented water. The Chinese travel writer Hiuen Tsang writes about the difficult, even violent, career of the tree—how King Sasanka, 'through envy, destroyed the convents and cut down the Bodhi Tree, digging it up to the very springs of the earth; but yet he did not get to the bottom of the roots. Then he burnt it with fire and sprinkled it with the juice of the sugarcane, desiring to destroy it entirely... Some months afterwards, the King of Magadha, called Purnavarma, the last of the race of Ashoka-raja, hearing of it, sighed and said, "The sun of wisdom having set, nothing is left but the tree of Buddha, and this they now have destroyed, what source of spiritual life is there now?" He then...with the milk of a thousand cows...bathed the roots of the tree, and in the night it once more revived and grew to the height of some 10 feet. Fearing lest it should be again cut down, he surrounded it with a wall of stone 24 feet high.' This violence towards a tree as if it were a human rival is to be found in all Buddhist literature about the Bodhi tree.

There were other discoveries I was making. I had, only a little while ago, learnt from a jolly Sri Lankan monk that the fig tree in Bodh Gaya was not unique to Gautama or our Sakyamuni Buddha. That, in fact, all the Buddhas before Gautama had had their own Bodhi trees—Vipassi had his trumpet flower tree, Sikhi the white mango tree, Vessabhu the sal, Krakuchhanda had his sirisa, Kanakmuni the udumbara, Kasyapa the banyan. Something interesting seemed to be happening here. The Hindu gods and goddesses had their own animals, called 'baahon' or vehicle. Durga had her lion, Lakshmi an owl, Saraswati a swan, Kartik had his peacock and Ganesh his mouse. Was this a deliberate—even revisionist—opposition, a subversion of the seemingly Hindu privileging of animal life over the plant?

There is something else to be said here. Just as the Buddha has had different incarnations, so has the Bodhi tree. The tree that I touched at Bodh Gaya is not the peepul tree under which Gautama found enlightenment. Alexander Cunningham believed that there ought to have been at least twenty generations of the peepul tree since Gautama first sat under it. G. P. Malalasekera's *Encyclopaedia of Buddhism* informs us that 'Buchanan who visited the site in 1811 saw the tree in full vigour and estimated its age as 100 years. Cunningham who visited the site in 1861 and 1871 found that during the 10 years the principal branches had disappeared and the stem was decaying fast. In 1876 during a storm the remaining parts of the Bodhi tree fell over the wall and there were the young sprouts to take the place of the dead tree, and thus came into being the Bodhi Tree at Buddha Gaya that exists at present.' Cunningham then ordered a cutting from the Bodhi Tree in Sri Lanka's Anuradhapura to be brought to Bodh Gaya—it is this tree that I saw being worshipped.

A branch had travelled with Ashoka's daughter, Sanghamitra, to Ceylon and inaugurated a new religion on the island, and birthed a tree that would become so central to its cultural and spiritual life that it would find place on the national flag of the island nation. More than a millennium later, a branch of the Sri Lankan tree had travelled back to Uruvela, bringing with it thousands of pilgrims from that island. If the Buddha was the tree, then the many reincarnations of the Buddha had its parallel in the many avatars of the Bodhi tree in different places in the Indian subcontinent. The continuing practice of 'distributing thirty two saplings obtained from this (Bodhi tree at Anuradhapura) tree and have them planted in thirty two selected sites' in Sri Lanka, as K. G. Senadeera tells us in his book, *Buddhist Symbolism of Wish-Fulfilment*, is another version of the many reincarnations of the tree, its many avatars.

There are other stories in Buddhist texts about trees. After a monk cut a branch by mistake, the spirit of the tree is supposed to have complained to the Buddha about losing her child. An instruction against cutting trees and its branches was immediately introduced into the monastic order. The *Bodhivamsa*, which gives us a detailed biography of the Bodhi tree, tells us about Ashoka's anxiety: how was he to lay a sword on the sacred Bodhi tree, and if he didn't, how would a branch of the tree reach Sri Lanka? This problem was eventually solved when a branch from the tree fell on its own, as the emperor sat contemplating a solution to the problem.

A tree cannot be cut because it stands for the Buddha. It *is* Buddha.

This metonymic relationship, the tree for the Buddha, I found fascinating, and I was curious to know what might have birthed this. There was little help from scholars on the subject. T. W. Rhys Davids, for instance, gives us this rather easy interpretation: 'In the old sculptures the Buddha Himself is never represented directly, but always under a symbol. What we have here then is reverence paid to the tree, not for its own sake, and not to any soul or spirit supposed to be in it, but to the tree either as the symbol of the Master, or because...it was under a tree of that kind that his followers believed that a venerated Teacher of old had become a Buddha.' The same sentiment about the seeming oneness of plants and people marks Buddhist teachings as well. The meritorious grow like an expansive banyan tree, those without merit remain short and stunted, like trees along the road.

The fig tree is associated with rain bearing and child bearing, and sometimes both have seemed like one and the same to me. K. G. Senadeera tells us that 'a deity called "*Kalu-devata-bandara*" is said to abide in this tree... Kalu is "black"—the colour of the rain cloud'. How fig trees affect the reproductive behaviour of clouds is a question for botanists and meteorologists, but some of the fertility rituals associated with the fig tree makes me wonder what the Buddha might have said about them. The Bodhi tree not only becomes a mother to a boy child, but is also said to hold inside it the destinies of kings. The flags of myths that move around it do not strike one as outrageous, only hoarsely imaginative. It apparently 'bleeds' when its nurturing community is in danger, a withering branch indicates a ruler's impending loss or death, and when a relative is ill people water the Bodhi tree seven times a day for seven days. In all this, the Bodhi tree stands in for a human, a king about to die, a sick relative, and so on.

The fig flower is mentioned in two chapters of the *Lotus Sutra*, and always in connection to the rare occurrence of both, the visible fig flower and the appearance of the Buddha in this world. Flower as the Buddha—Thich Nhat Hanh also makes the same comparison when he says, 'The udumbara flower, although fallen from the stem, is still fragrant'. The fragrance of the flower is not lost with its severing from the tree, and so our potential for enlightenment. A web commentary on this passage from Hanh brings the lay person's assessment to the foreground: 'The Buddha taught that everyone is a Buddha, everyone is an udumbara flower.'

It is a bit strange to come to a description of the Buddha's physical appearance after all this, and after all the images and statues, I turn to the A,I:181, and there he is, our Gautama likened to a tree: 'It is wonderful, truly marvellous, how serene is the good Gautama's appearance, how clear and radiant his complexion, just as the golden jujube in autumn is clear and radiant, just as a palm-tree fruit just loosened from the stalk is clear and radiant ...'

> Buddha is dead.
> But, if you meet the Buddha,
> don't invent another god
> or behead another demon; just
> sip some tea under a tree.

So goes a short Buddhist poem by Zen master Linji Yixuan.

Wasn't this the same philosophy that had marked the Buddha's words to his disciple Ananda, about the Bodhi tree being a substitute for his own person? Ananda Coomaraswamy, one of the most important philosophers in the field, had marked this person-for-the-plant relationship as special too: 'What is especially noteworthy is the designation of the single fig tree as the world-form of one awakener ... for just also is the Buddha's fig tree being the chosen symbol of the Buddha's unseen essence. It is an enduring basis for the vision of the Buddha'. You can't see the Buddha, but you can see the tree. You cannot be blessed by the Buddha, you can sit under the shade of the tree. Buddhism, at least in my practical understanding of its origin and practice, is a religion of self-centredness, in ways both good and bad. In asking its practitioners to limit its focus to oneself, it asks us to become trees. K. G. Senadeera writes, 'A Bhikkhu who enters the courtyard of a Bodhi tree should venerate the tree behaving with humility as if he were in the presence of the Buddha himself.'.

And so I grew certain that the Buddha was a tree, an evergreen tree.

I had told myself that I was going to Bodh Gaya to discover the effect of sitting under a tree, to see whether it abetted detachment, this special tree, for the Bodhi tree is the real celebrity in Bodh Gaya. But the bureaucracy around the tree, with fort-like walls protecting it from touches and sittings, had denied me that experience. That disappointment, however, had disappeared, at least temporarily, when I discovered from a Thai monk a piece of information that might have been useless to him. We had been discussing the sculptures of the Bodhi tree at Barhut, when he suddenly mentioned Cunningham on four 'guardian spirits' of the tree—Venu, Valgu, Ojopati.

The fourth guardian spirit was called Sumana.

Part IX

The Tree is an Eternal Corpse
—Srijato, *'Marjonashopan'*

THE DEATH OF TREES

Trees do not die in slow motion. When they fall it is a traumatic event. Maya Angelou was recognizing exactly that trauma in her poem, 'When Great Trees Fall':

> When great trees fall,
> rocks on distant hills shudder,
> lions hunker down
> in tall grasses,
> and even elephants
> lumber after safety.

Unlike humans, the plant world knows at least two kinds of life expectancy. There are the annual, even seasonal, plants, flowering prodigiously in spring or summer before their Keatsian death. In our minds, their overwhelming beauty is often allied to their short lifespan, and this is quite different from the sense of tragic loss that attends the death of ancient trees. A dead tree is, for me, a reminder of the gracelessness of death. For when a tree dies and falls to the ground, one realizes the redundancy of a pillow.

On 25 April 2015, an uncharacteristically gloomy and overcast day, just around noon, an earthquake struck Siliguri. My husband was the first to rush downstairs, to open doors and gates so that his father and I could follow. My father-in-law is seventy-nine, and, fortunately, fit for his age. But as the staircase shook and moved like a river in spate, he found himself unable to trust land anymore. I pulled and dragged

him by the hand, but he resisted—fear had paralysed his mind and then later his feet. By the time I managed to pull him out of the compound and on to the street where a crowd of earthquake exiles chattered excitedly about the quake, the tremors had stopped. And then it began again. We watched our house shaking—it was slightly tragicomic, the chandelier on the terrace moving like a swing, the windows chattering, the doors suddenly acquiring automatism. Right in front of the building, a kamini tree, nearly as old as my husband, swayed as well. A long branch held itself out, a visual gift of a bunch of much loved yellow flowers. When the second of the earthquakes came, and we rushed back out on to the street once again, I noticed, almost by accident, that only one flower remained on the tree where there had been nine. The rest hadn't been able to resist the earthquake's pull.

It was impossible to do much that day. My legs continued to shake long after the ground had stopped shaking. Along with the sight of my father-in-law's panic-stricken face, I could not forget a couple of other things—first, the guilt of abandoning all my plants in the house, even as I did not forget to pick up the cell phone to call my parents to find out where they were; the second was my thoughtlessness about the quake affecting trees. We worry about the effect of natural disasters on human beings, animals, buildings, but how little we care about their effect on trees!

⁂

When my mother-in-law died, my husband refused to follow the Hindu rituals associated with mourning the dead. It made his relatives angry—their rhetoric was rural. They would be ostracized by society for this disobedience, they said. My husband, exhausted by tempestuous sadness, refused to argue. He had decided that his period of grief would not be restricted to a fortnight of forced mourning. And so he did not wear the white dhoti and cotton shawl, he did not walk on bare feet, he shaved every morning, he cut his nails every Sunday, and on the eleventh day, he did not get his head tonsured.

Our marriage was still new, and in my effort to be a useful partner, especially in those circumstances, I became his unappointed advocate. And so in my amateurish way, I tried to remind them of the sociological origins of these rituals, how they were all a part of the process of letting the world know about the deceased. Why do you have a beard? Why is your head tonsured? Why these clothes? The answer was the Hindu body itself, it was performing the role of what bureaucracy would later turn into the death certificate.

For eleven days after what was a—how does one say it without lavish sentimentality?—life-altering experience for my husband, he battled instructions from these well-meaning people, but there were moments when grief collapsed into rage. During one such moment, he pointed towards me and made what might have sounded like a speech to this group of people.

'My wife weeps when a plant dies. For lack of watering, from a gardener's indifference, from a woodcutter's greed... At first, I used to mock what I considered an unnecessary sentimentality. Only now do I understand how she feels,' he said.

His eldest uncle intercepted. 'A mother and a tree are not the same thing...'

'You don't need to tell that to a son who's just lost his mother,' my husband replied. 'My wife does not wear white clothes when she grieves for her dead plants.'

I was touched by his words but also saddened by the tradition it belonged to. For this had struck me even when I was still very little— why are there no traditions to mourn dead plant life?

And why are there no obituaries written for dead trees?

🌱

I have been to an astrologer only once in my life. I had been unwell for months, and in spite of doctors and their diagnoses and prescriptions, some ailment or the other would return. My parents are tolerant agnostics, but my brother, always quietly rebellious, stunned us all by becoming a devout believer in any knowledge system that offered a pathway out of pain and trouble, and, of course, uncertainty. One of the most uncomplicated people I know, his reasoning is simple: every system should be allowed the benefit of trial and error. My brother insisted and then later compelled me to accompany him to an astrologer. Moved by his affection, I went along.

I do not regret anything about that evening. I was expecting to return grumpy and annoyed, with a long list of prescribed gems and precious stones for cure but my experience was quite the opposite. The 'astrologer' we met was everything that I'd never expected an astrologer to be: we spoke about geography, which seemed to be his pet interest, about his obsession for knowledge about the latitudinal and longitudinal position of a place before visiting it as a child; we also spoke about rivers, and pollution, and towards the end of the hour, he spoke sadly about noise pollution. I was momentarily charmed. He recommended nothing for me, saying I was perfect the way I was. 'Some people are prone to diseases just as some are more prone to making wise investments in business,' he said.

A few years would pass before I felt the need to see him again. It had been a terrible summer and my plants had found it difficult to survive the heat. I grew more attentive to their needs, watered them more frequently, fed them plant food, and even cured the soil. The gardener was more worried about his job than he was about the plants. For years we'd shared this relationship of happy dissent: he addressed my amateur's worries with scorn and sarcasm, and when I brought to him my mix of textbookish knowledge with what to him seemed like an excess of emotion, he would try and deflect my discourse into anecdotal evidence of his skills. When it seemed like all our efforts would come to naught, and that there would be a sea of dead plants on my terrace, the gardener blurted out what he said had been on his mind for a long time: 'Something must be wrong with the horoscope of these plants.'

Coincidences are difficult to explain. I happened to run into Bappada, the astrologer, a few days after the gardener's pronouncement about the plants' horoscopes. It was at a plant nursery by the Mahananda River in our town. The Pradhans, who owned the nursery, were old acquaintances, their daughter and I had studied in the same school, she graduating a year after me. I'd come to them with the hope that they would be the plant doctors I so urgently needed. Entering the gated compound, I found Bappa-da, an orchid in one hand, his bike helmet in the other. When he enquired after my health, I told him instead about the failing health of my plants. I was taken aback by his reply: 'You are ailing because your plants are ailing.'

I told him about our gardener, his demand that horoscopes for all our houseplants be made, that astrology be invoked to save the plants. Did I really believe that that was possible? he asked me, smiling. I told him I didn't, and yet which parent will not cross over to the other side of reason to save her offspring? Bappa-da is a patient man, and when I think of it now, I can only admire his tolerance of me that Sunday morning. Death is not a happy subject for discussion, but it is, without a doubt, a deeply involving one. My fears crept out—I told him that I constantly worried about the fate of my plants after my death. How was I to leave all that I owned to my plants? We laughed together, Bappa-da and I, and after Mrs Pradhan had suggested to me a few tips with which to re-energize my plants, he asked me whether I'd read Syed Mustafa Siraj's short stories about plant life. I hadn't.

Later that day, when I mentioned it to my husband, he gave me an ancient copy of Mustafa Siraj's stories. It had, I made out from the inscription, belonged to my mother-in-law. On the last page was her handwriting in green ink: 'I can't walk anymore. I can't go to people. People come to me. I have become a tree.'

Most remarkable among Mustafa Siraj's stories on plant life is 'Gachhta Boleychhilo', The Tree Said. In a village is a tree that bears no fruits or flowers, a tree utterly unremarkable—'an orphan, an untouchable, lonely and without any caste, illiterate, a greedy tree', a tree so hopeless that 'no one has even wanted to commit suicide by hanging from its branches'. The villagers might have been interested to find out its name had it been a more attractive plant, but they show absolutely no curiosity in finding out the race and caste of this tree.

There was only one thing to separate this tree from the rest. That was its untree-like behaviour. This was a speaking tree. Not everyone could hear it speak, though. Like dogs who only can hear subsonic sounds, this tree's words were audible only to those who would soon die. And the tree's vocabulary was pretty limited: 'Mawr, mawr, mawr...' 'Mawr' in Bangla could have two meanings: one is 'die'; the other is onomatopoeic, the creaking sound of trees and wooden objects that are about to break or collapse. When a poor old woman went near the tree to scavenge for dried leaves, the tree said, 'Mawr, mawr, mawr.' The woman, who was petrified with fear to find herself near a speaking tree, one cursing her to death, died instantly. An old villager corroborated this—'Some trees can speak. Some trees are angry and have a temper, some are cruel and wicked'. If trees spoke in the dialect of the wind, what was 'Mawr, mawr, mawr'? The answer arrived from carriers of 'ancient wisdom': 'Just as some birds manage to pick up the languages of men, so can some trees.'

But the world was full of cynics, says the narrator; and disbelievers. And so men went and threatened the tree, taunted it, even kicked it. In return, the tree only used its monosyllabic vocabulary—'mawr'. And the men died the next day.

The tree lived in what the narrator repeatedly calls 'no man's land'. Children loved it unconditionally, without expectation of fruit or flower. The tree loved them back and did them no harm. It did not curse. Speculation about the paranormal behaviour of the tree produced several theses: perhaps ghosts and witches had made a home in it, who could tell? Or perhaps a cross-pollination of several religions had turned it thus? For apart from the ostentatious rituals of Hindu worship and the crowded processions on Eid and Muharram, the new religion of voting, with its intolerable loudspeakers, was changing the moral and sound ecology of the village. 'The tree was an out and out proletariat whose idea of discipline was in taming its branches and roots. It had nothing to lose.'

Politicians were quick to spot an opportunity in turning this into an election issue: gossip circulated about one party bribing the old woman to die. Amidst such mischief, Panu the thief, who had sought a hiding place in the neighbourhood of the cursing tree, heard the same utterance. 'Mawr, mawr, mawr.' He died soon after. The police arrived, led by an inspector who was an agnostic. Their enquiry did

Sumana Roy

not turn up much except that the panchayat, in an unprecedented gesture, declared the tree 'dangerous'. A petition against the felling of the tree began to circulate in the village.

All this, of course, comes only after the death of the young doctor, who, newly arrived from the city, heartbroken in young love, had often spoken about committing suicide. He had taunted the tree saying: 'Hello Brihanala! What do you say? What about me? Don't you understand English? Okay. Do you understand Bangla? Tell me what is it that you want to tell me.'

The tree had replied in the only language it knew: 'Mawr, mawr, mawr'.

A suicide note was discovered next to the young doctor's dead body the next morning. 'No one is responsible for my death.'

When a villager repeats the young doctor's taunt, calling the tree Brihanala, someone neither man nor woman, after Arjun's guise as a third gender person in the Mahabharata, a chorus of 'Mawr, mawr, mawr' surrounds the village. Bombs explode. There is blood in no man's land.

Why had the astrologer asked me to read this story? Could it be that he was trying to tell me about the relationship between trees and death from the other side of the lens? I do not know what Mustafa Siraj's story *means*, I also do not know whether trees have their own languages and dialects. What Bappa-da probably wanted me to do was to walk to the other side of grief and not see trees only as suffering victims.

In another story, an old man, who could be called both farmer and gardener, waits for his youngest son at a village railway station every night. His wife is dead, as is his eldest child, who died of snakebite. This son is all he has, but the world around him is annoyed with the poor man's affection for the office-going son. His son too has almost no use for the father's extravagant emotions, apart from when it serves his practical needs—the old man is an efficient housekeeper. A female friend from the city will visit him in the village, the son informs the old man one day. The father must not call him by his nickname, he must not do anything that gives away the fact that he is the man's father—'I'll call you father a thousand times later to make up for the day.' He is to pretend to be a 'mali', a professional gardener, so that he does not embarrass his citified son who finds everything about his father displeasing.

The son is embarrassed about his father. There is, first, the old man's appearance: 'a wild man's body, the dirty dhoti pulled up to his knees, a dirty rag like *gamchha* on his shoulder. He bends forward when he walks. This wasn't age, it was the force of the earth. The attraction for the earth, the soil, had given him a hunchback. All his life he had moved from the surface of the earth to its deepest force field. Sasthicharan would never be able to stand up straight again. He was a gardener'. Then there was the language. When he tried to engage his son in a conversation, the retort came most often like this: 'Go. Go dig up the earth. You won't understand anything else.' And so when his son, now only a weekend visitor, having made arrangements to live in the city on workdays, asks him to behave like the son's employee for a day, the old man feels like he has turned into an immobile tree—he can only wave his hands, like the branches of a tree.

The city girl, Mustafa Siraj takes pains to inform us, is attractive in a way the old man finds fascinating, even intimidating. She brings her textbook knowledge to the garden. 'A Prince Albert rose grows in a village such as this one?' 'Mali, don't you grow rajnigandha here?' The son, wishing to impress her, mimics the tone one reserves for a subordinate: 'Old man, what flowers are those, those with the thin white petals?' When Sasthicharan tells them that those flowers are eaten, the girl's quick exclamation follows: 'Really? Even flowers are eaten, can you believe that?'

Who is this girl, Sasthicharan wonders, who has filled this ancient quiet of his garden, his 'boba baagan', his mute garden, with this quick-spirited restlessness, with joy, with rhythm, with health and laughter and youth and tunefulness? Suddenly she chances upon the gardener's face where years of 'cobwebs, beastly rivers, insect teeth, bird nests' have melted into tears. 'Why are you crying, why O Gardener? Sugata, look your old gardener is crying.'

Disturbed by the possibility of the truth erupting with those tears, he explains, 'The old man is mad. He cries sometimes.' When Ritu, the woman, (her name means season), wonders aloud whether it is a 'psychological problem', he gives her a backstory: 'A long time ago, a snakebite killed his son. You can imagine how it must have been—first, this village, then this jungle. Since then the old man's turned half mad.'.

What follows is unimaginable. Sasthicharan picks up a sharp gardening tool, the khurpi, and shouts, 'Beware!...Go away, leave immediately. Run. Or I'll kill you...kill you.'

The young lovers run away, the son in amazement, his woman in fear.

The story is titled 'Pushpobonay Hotyakando', Murder in the Flower Garden.

From this one I moved curiously, even greedily, to one titled 'Shaakkhibawt', The Banyan as Witness. In a village where life still moves to the taut rhythms of class, caste and convention, a young man from a lower caste becomes romantically involved with a Brahmin widow. Expectedly, this relationship must come to a sanguinary end. The young man is killed and the young widow goes missing. The relationship, its curation and culmination, culpability and climax, takes place under an ancient banyan, and hence the title, the tree as patriarch, as witness. I use the word 'patriarch' with good reason—for when the story ends, we find the missing woman under her father-in-law's protection.

The girl is often referred to as 'the girl from Sundori-tala', meaning the girl from under the sundori tree. The patronage of the tree is crucial to the moral of the story. In the end, the old father asks the outsider Makhan-babu, 'You tell me, did I do the right thing?' I quote the rest. 'Makhan-babu said—the right thing. Then he suddenly remembered the familiar banyan. Surrounded by many green crowns, its dark branches and numerous aerial roots stands the village banyan. Underneath is its shade. But at the moment the tree has suddenly begun to look like a man...' This is Mustafa Siraj turning a folk tale inside out—the dead human lover returns to protect, sometimes as man, at other times as tree.

It is indeed curious, this relationship between death and plant life, in these stories. 'Ekti Pistol O Dumur Gachh', A Pistol and a Fig Tree, is set in a village like the other two stories. In it lives a young man called 'Boka', whose name literally means 'Fool'. Scared of being killed by a rival family in the village, Boka, once a naive and innocent boy, has bought a pistol to protect himself. Untrained in its use, he becomes an autodidact. His 'target' for practice is an ancient fig tree. It is 'older than the grandfather of our grandfathers—it is ancient and meditative in its appearance. My grandfather was a railway employee. He would come to this verandah close to the fig tree and say that all the peace in this world was here'. The narrator, an old friend of Boka's, watches him shoot at the tree where he once somersaulted on summer afternoons. It saddens him to see Boka turn this good-natured old tree into an enemy. And yet he rails: 'Let that fig tree stand in for your enemy. Shoot right through it.'

The narrator's consciousness moves between Boka and the tree. So immediately after that imploration to Boka, he says, 'Perhaps trees understand everything. I felt I saw the tree smiling in a meditative poise. Come my child, I'm waiting with my chest left open for you. Practice as much as you want to.' He feels the tree's spirit for martyrdom: 'I am very fond of the fig tree. It is ready to help protect Boka. That is the thing about rural trees. They give you shade. They give you fruits. They give you oxygen all day. And they offer themselves as targets willingly. C'mon Boka, shoot, I am ready.'

A police team arrives at the spot where Boka had been honing his shooting skills. They look at the wounds on the lone victim—the poor fig tree—and leave. The narrator's sister-in-law tells him about Boka's romantic and sexual escapades with a girl called Thumri under the same fig tree. That night everyone wakes up to the sound of an explosion. Morning brings the news of Boka's death, he being killed by his enemies.

After the news had unsettled the day, the narrator visits the fig tree. 'Like a crown over the water hyacinth pond, the fig tree stands like it always did—meditative in its poise and indifferent. Old man, you've failed. You left your heart and body open, but it came to naught.' When he gets closer to the tree, he finds Thumri staring at the tree, her eyes swollen with grief.

An angry Jesus had cursed a fig tree: Remain barren and childless.

Sumana Roy

Ramlochan Mohanta's daughter, Thumri, was cursing the tree: Tui mawr! Tui mawr! Tui mawr! You die! You die! You die!

⚘

Alain de Botton's *The Pleasures and Sorrows of Work* brought the work of Stephen Taylor to the world. For three years Taylor, unable to come to terms with the deaths of a close friend and his parents, painted an oak tree—the stories of the art of those three years are now available to us in Taylor's book, *Oak: One Tree, Three Years, Fifty Paintings*. 'Tell me what you see vanishing and I will tell you who you are,' wrote the American poet W. S. Merwin. In Taylor's paintings one notices the life of a 250-year-old oak and its seeming unchangeability when viewed against human time and the fast-time notions of death. Why did the man paint the same tree from different angles and perspectives every day for more than a thousand days? Taylor's answer has to do with the permanence of aged trees when compared to our short lives: 'You lose your sense of identity when you lose friends and family and I suddenly didn't know who I was. I walked into this field one day and just sat down and started to paint. I painted the tree from every angle, in oils and watercolours, I drew it and photographed it. At the time I didn't think about why I was doing it, but looking back now I think I was trying to feel at home. I had lost everything that anchored me... It was a mid-life crisis brought about by the repeated deaths of important people in my life that I was coping with... The oak has a feeling of permanence. You find it crops up a lot in the paintings of Constable, in Virginia Woolf's *Orlando* and also in *War and Peace*, where it takes on a symbolic meaning. I'm alright now, but I think by taking this one little area of England and feeding off it spiritually I found some redemption.'

Trees are not immortal, of course, but the death of trees by 'natural causes', as post-mortem reports of humans often declare, causes much less mourning in us than the murder of trees. The same economy of emotion seems to operate here—advanced age is a natural invocator to death in our minds, but an untimely end is emotionally draining. And hence the endless—and timeless—parables about the immorality in killing trees.

How I Became a Tree

THE REBIRTH OF TREES

It seems so natural, in dreams and folk tales, that humans should be reborn as trees. On a bus to nowhere, I sat next to a man who had dressed like a TV version of a sage in red robes, a dhoti and a bandana-like piece of cloth with which he had gathered his locks of matted hair into a bundle on the top of his head.

He began speaking to me.

'I recognize a soulmate when I see one,' he said.

I wasn't sure whether he was speaking to me, and so I ignored him.

'You and I were neighbours once,' he continued.

I turned to look at him. No, he did not look like someone whose face I had ever spotted in a neighbouring window.

'You must be making a mistake,' I said.

'Not in this life,' he smiled, raising his hands above his head to indicate something.

I didn't answer. But that was no relief. For he wasn't finished.

'We were neighbours in Baikanthapur Forest. Don't you remember anything at all? You were a sal tree. And so was I.' The man waited for a response but I wasn't going to oblige him, and as soon as I could I got off the bus. But his words had found their mark.

I was tempted to contemplate my past life as a sal tree. To want to be a tree was one thing; to be told that I'd already lived that life was another. Over the next few days, I moved between looking at the sal-wood furniture in the house and reading anxiously about trees and their mechanisms of rebirth. The Rig Veda has a hymn to Agni, the fire god, which the dead man can overhear: 'May your eye go to the sun, your life's breath to the wind, Go to the sky or to earth, as is your nature; or go to the waters, if that is your fate. Take root in the plants with your limbs'. Ellison Banks Findly in her book, *Plant Lives: Borderline Beings in Indian Traditions*, tells us that when Jaratkarava Artabhaga asks Yajnavalkya in the Brihadaranyaka Upanishad, about what happens to a human after his death, he explains it thus: among other things, 'hairs of the body to the herbs (*osadhi*), hairs on the head to the trees (*vanaspati*)...' This repeated analogy between human hair and plant life in the Vedas and Upanishads took me back to the number of times I compared the autumnal fall of leaves to my hair fall. (It had come to me through my amateurish etymology—'*rukkho*', the word for dry skin or hair seemed to me a relative of '*rookh*', the Hindi word for tree.) The Aitareya Upanishad describes the cosmic person as one from whose hair come plants and trees. The Brihadaranyaka Upanishad tells us that a dead person's hair was to be distributed among plants. Even pubic hair becomes a part of this train of logic—it turns into kusa, grass. And just as we believe that hair is not hurt when it is cut, so too with grass, which the Vedic thinkers tell us, must be placed on the spot where the axe will strike a tree so that it is not hurt. This idea of being part of a great recycling chain where I could be several things seemed like a fun idea at first. Banks Findly's words came as comfort and indulgence: 'The Upanishadic view of the great person cycling through the cosmos and emerging from plants as food for those on earth is reflected in a passage from the Mahabharata.' She then quotes from a telling passage in the epic where Dhaumya says this to Yudhishthira: 'When the creatures were first created, they suffered great hunger, and in his compassion for them the Sun acted like a father. Going his northern course he absorbed with his rays the saps of heat; then, on returning to his southern course, the Sun impregnated the earth. Thereupon, when he had become the fields, the Lord of the Herbs collected the heat from heaven, and, with the water, engendered the herbs. Thus the Sun, having gone unto earth, and ejaculated by the fervors of the moon, is born as the herbs of the six flowers, which are sacrificial, and thus is he born as the food of the living ones on earth.'

Even the gods and their enemies have experienced this cycle of rebirth. Banks Findly tells us about Vritra, Indra's enemy, who is turned into a plant after violence is inflicted upon him—'a broken reed', 'a tree whose branches have been lopped off by an axe', 'the dead Vritra is compared to violated plants'. The demons in the Ramayana fall down 'deformed and deprived of their lives, (lying) on the ground like trees whose roots have been severed'.

Hans-Peter Schmidt, in a fine essay on the origin of non-violence, quotes from the *Satapatha Brahmana* to make an important point about the idea of rebirth that was common at the time: 'Whatever food a man consumes in this world, that (food), in return, consumes him in yonder world.' Schmidt gives the example of 'a woodcutter who once cut a tree is now a tree being cut by a woodcutter who was once the first tree being cut' and 'a man who once ate a plant is now a plant being eaten by a man who once was the first plant being eaten'. And hence the short prayer by woodcutters before they put their axe to a tree or even grass cutters, as this quote from the *Satapatha Brahmana* illustrates:

> 'O earth, that affordest the place for making offerings to the gods! May I not injure the root of thy plant!'... Whilst he takes up (the earth dug up by the sword), he thus addresses her: 'May I not injure the roots of thy plants!'

Lance E. Nelson, in an essay in *Purifying the Earthly Body of God: Religion and Ecology in Hindu India*, writes about bad karma resulting in one's birth as a tree: 'As the result of evil karma, souls are born as plants, which endure suffering when they are harvested, cooked, and eaten... Trees and other plants... serve as bodies in which the results of sins may be experienced through reincarnation.' This low—perhaps lowest—place in the karma-meter owes to plants being deprived of the much glorified five senses.

Ellison Banks Findly draws up a random list of people turning to trees after their death:

> There is an early report of rebirth as a plant in the Atharva Veda,

Sumana Roy

that tells of an asuri or demoness who takes the shape of a forest tree in order to make a remedy for leprosy. Shakti Gupta records various later Hindu stories: the myth of Parvati cursing some gods to be reborn as trees; a Gadaba tribal story of five sisters (Mango, Tamarind, Fig, Jamun, and Plantain) who are reborn as trees when their husbands run away in fright at the great number of children that they bear; a post-Portuguese legend of an ugly princess who kills herself and produces a tobacco plant from her cremated ashes; and the myth of Tulasi who, in the wake of atrocities committed by her husband, becomes a sati, giving rise to the Vaisnava-sacred Tulsi (basil) plant from her pyre. Pandey notes the myth of Surya Bai, daughter of the sun, who, to escape persecution from a sorceress, becomes a golden lotus; when the flower is burnt to the ground by the sorceress, a mango tree emerges from the ashes, and from the ripe fruit Surya Bai emerges again. And the Majupurias record the folktale of a minister's daughter becoming a Campaka tree with golden flowers.

This recycling technology of rebirth must have some grounding in certainty—why do these suffering victims become trees and not something else, an animal or even another person? Was there some kind of guarantee—some certainty—about the system of rebirth? Was it a system at all? Or was it completely random, these creatures we became in other births? All responses to these wayward questions must remain only in the nature of speculation because of our sad lack of knowledge about our other lives. Except for those fortunate—and unfortunate—few who have inherited memories from a past life. I grew curious about such atavistic knowledge.

Buddhist and Jain literature tells us that rebirths as plants and trees are not exclusively happy experiences. In the *Uttaradhyayana*, a person recollects his torturous life as a tree, of a life of perennial anxiety, of being torn and broken, of the pains on his body. In the *Tattvartha Sutra*, another recounts his life as a salmali tree—'as a tree I have been felled, slit, sawn into planks, and stripped of the bark by carpenters with axes, hatchets, etc., an infinite number of times'.

Did I still want to be a tree?

🌱

As I have mentioned earlier in the book, the tales of transformation of humans into trees from Ovid's *Metamorphoses* had stoked, even fanned, my need to turn into a tree. In most of them I found women—even men—turning into trees to escape from violence. It was the same impulse, emotional more than physical, that had ignited my desire to turn into a tree. Then there are the folk tales in which men and women die to be reborn as trees. There is the tale about two brothers finding two beautiful fish in a stream, bringing them home, only to find them turn into women. They marry the women, but the older brother, who had burnt one of the fish while preparing to cook it, desires the younger brother's wife because his wife's face bears scars of the burns. He makes several attempts to kill his brother and eventually succeeds, when he traps the young man inside a cave in a forest. Months pass by, the younger brother dies of starvation, but his wife refuses to believe her brother-in-law when he says her husband is dead. So he takes her to the cave to show her his dead body. The woman locks the door of the cave from inside immediately and eventually perishes there. The older brother's wife, who had grown suspicious about her husband's activities, had followed him into the forest. When she visits the cave a few days later, she finds two trees locked in a lover's embrace. It does not take her long to understand that these are the younger brother and his wife, now reborn as trees. She takes a leaf from one of the trees and wipes her face with it. Though she can't see it then, the scars from the burns vanish, and this makes her husband suspicious—he stabs her to death. The woman turns into a bird and finds shelter in the trees.

Turning into a tree seems a safe enough shelter for the dead who want to remain alive in some way. There are versions and variations of this tale in all cultures. The most recent among them is Robert Coover's story, 'The Crabapple Tree', about the human-tree metamorphosis. A woman dies during childbirth leaving her son, called Dickie-boy, in her husband's care. The man drank too much, and since no other woman in the neighbourhood would have him, he married a woman who refused to socialize with anyone. People called her the Vamp for the ways in which she manipulated men and also because 'she'd taken half the men in town to bed'. Vamp had a daughter, Marleen, from a previous marriage, and she soon became a play companion to Dickie-boy whose father loved and resented him because the little boy reminded him of his dead wife.

Dickie-boy seemed to have magical powers about him—he once climbed up to the top of the crabapple tree and the Fire Brigade had to be called to rescue him. His stepsister said that it was the crabapple tree that helped him to get to the top—his mother had, after all, been buried under the tree. Another time Marleen wanted a dog and Dickie-boy became a dog, almost a real dog. Such uncanny incidents were routine at their place. Dickie-boy had many gifts—one of these was a knack for finding lost things. But he died soon. Although the police couldn't find any evidence against the Vamp, everyone was convinced that the woman had killed the stepson she couldn't stand. He was promptly buried under the crabapple tree. His father soon followed him there. The Vamp developed some kind of mental illness and she became scared of everything, particularly the crabapple tree.

Marleen, who inherited the estate, turned it into a wildlife range, dug up her stepbrother's bones to bring him back to life, or that at least was what she told her playmates. 'To protect the tree, Marleen had an extension built onto the farmhouse, with a hole in the roof for the tree, or perhaps it moved in on its own. Its apples were said to be poisonous, but birds gathered in its laden branches like twittering harpies to eat them, and, if anything, they got louder and bigger, and there were more of them than ever.'

It took me time, so carried away was I with my obsession, to realize that all these transformations were steeped in, caused by or resulted in violence, particularly to women. Rape, murder or wilful death. Is a human dying to be born as a tree an escape from human cruelty?

※

A tree has more afterlives than a man. Firewood and furniture are two that are most common. As I watched wood put through manicuring processes in a sawmill beside my house, I grew nervous about an imagined afterlife when more powerful beings might scrape off my skin and hair and toes and intestines to make me suitable for their utilitarian needs.

The supposedly painless ease with which dead trees allowed themselves to become the props and accompaniments to our lives made me angry on their behalf.

Trees do not deserve this. They do not commit crimes. And yet they are given capital punishment.

Do men kill trees the way they kill fellow humans? What is the difference between the two assassinations? Animals might kill plants for food, man is the only animal that kills trees for wood. Early childhood brings us versions of 'The Giving Tree', a story about a relationship between a little boy and a tree. The Bengali writer, Narayan Sanyal, adapted it with illustrations for children in Bengal with a few tweaks—'The Giving Tree' became 'Gachh Ma', meaning Tree Mother, and the apples of the American poet and writer Shel Silverstein's 1964 illustrated story book became mangoes to aid the Bengali child's familiarity quotient. A little boy loves the mango tree and grows up playing with it—making a crown of fallen mango leaves to become the king of forests, swinging on its branches, climbing up its trunk, playing hide-and-seek, resting against it when tired, and of course, feeding on its mangoes, sour mangoes, sweet mangoes, unripe mangoes, ripe mangoes, overripe mangoes.

But days passed by and the boy, called here by the generic name 'Khoka', grew up. The Tree Mother missed him. Suddenly he appeared one day, asking the mango tree for money. The Tree Mother asked the young man to collect and then sell the mangoes. Many years passed. The man, not young anymore, returned to the tree—he was in need of money again. The Tree Mother asked him to chop off her branches which the man did promptly and left. Again, many years passed. The man, now aged, returned, and this time too, asked for money. The Tree Mother asked him to cut off her trunk which the man did easily, without guilt. And then the man returned again but the tree had nothing else to give him anymore. So the man went and sat on its chopped trunk. Around him was barren terrain where there had once been a neighbourhood of trees. Angry at the lack of any shade from the scorching sun, he suddenly noticed a little boy planting saplings. The Tree Mother had lost her eyes but not her ears. She was happy to see that she had managed to help the little boy again.

Killing a mother must rank as one of the most abominable crimes among humans. But the murder of a Tree Mother at the hands of an ungrateful son breeds only a passing contempt in us. Mahasweta Devi, who spent her life writing about the marginalized, critiques this difference in her popular story, 'Arjun'. Set in a village that runs largely on a timber economy, the illegal felling associated with it brings out the difference we make between the killing of humans and trees. 'At the end of the day I need some money. If you tell me to cut a tree, I'll cut a tree, if you ask me to cut a man, I'll cut a man.'

'If you are born in Purulia, it's a rule that you'll kill trees in the jungle; it's also a rule that you'll have to go to jail for that.' Caught between a government which punishes the locals for cutting trees and a timber mafia which punishes them for not cutting trees, the tribals suffer. An arjun tree must be cut, a timber merchant orders one day, this against the background of forthcoming elections. But this is a special tree, sacred to the village. 'When it was young, people would worship beneath its shade before setting out on hunts. Even in old age, it is so beautiful. A whitish body, its head in the skies, the full moon dissolves all difference between the moonlight and the tree... Gradually they begin to see that the arjun tree suffers from the same fate as them.' Elections and their voting machinery are a terror. The arjun tree is turned into a 'graam debota', the village deity—tribals from the neighbourhood arrive with drums and music to worship it. The timber and vote merchants are defeated, at least temporarily. 'The leaves of the arjun tree resemble the human tongue.'

HOW I BECAME A TREE

Outside my bedroom window is a papaya tree. It is like a mother to me—I take it for granted like I do my mother. This is not a lazy simile—our blindness to plants is pervasive and widespread. As I've said earlier, I'd spent much energy on recording the responses of a variety of plants and trees to the wind—the leaves of the bamboo and the mango, grass and the jackfruit. But I hadn't recorded the reaction of papaya leaves to a strong wind. One windy day in April, during a northwester, I sat by the giant windows of my bedroom that I'd partially cracked open, and watched the papaya tree. The hand-shaped papaya leaves, with their finger-like sharp extensions, became defensive against the wind, the edges of the leaves curling in on themselves. After some time, the direction of the wind changed and I felt my hair running away from me. My hands came to my rescue, an ineffectual shield. I realized that my hands were behaving in almost exactly the same manner as the papaya leaves.

As I sat there, trying to deal with the gale, I looked at the bones of my hands, hidden under the skin, but rising into prominence as I moved my fingers. I thought then of bones and wondered what would happen if I were able to break my bones and rearrange them into the shape of a tree.

Nandalal Bose's drawing of a V-shaped twig, adjacent to a human elbow, came to me. I continued with my thought experiment, excitement coursing through me. Nothing about my human structure seemed precious to me—not even the bilateral symmetry where so much of human beauty comes from. In my head, my two hands, two feet, two shoulders, all of these pairs were broken to create—fit into—a trunk from which smaller branches emanated. The smallest of twigs I conjured out of an assemblage of my little fingers. It was not difficult to imagine skin as bark. Winter's discontent and dehydration would take care of that.

I am conscious that my thoughts turn towards death often, looking at it for a cure, for it to fulfil the blank spaces on the canvas of this life. This explains the scale of my investment in the afterlife. I speculate inconsequentially about whether trees commit suicide and whether there are tree martyrs. On the Internet I find a Spanish design studio by the name of Estudi Moliné that can turn the after-death ashes of humans and other animals into a tree: 'Bios Urn changes the way people see death, converting the "end of life" into a transformation and a return to life through nature. [It is] a smart, sustainable, and ecologically friendly way to approach what's, probably, one of the most important moments in human life.' Divided into two capsules, the top half for the seed and the lower half for the ashes, the seed begins to take root independently once the urn breaks down. I also find something similar called Capsula Mundi, the invention of two Italian designers, Anna Citelli and Raoul Bretzel: 'Leaving behind a tree definitely seems like a better option than leaving behind a tombstone,' their website declares.

I'd choose to be an Ashoka, the a-shoka, the sorrowless tree, I decide.

I had once imagined my encounter with death as the equivalent of having grains of sand inside my mouth. That sand now moves south from my mouth to my feet, my roots. For much of my life, I am aware that I have tried to replicate the habits and actions of those who'd wanted, even if temporarily, to live like trees—by sitting under trees, making love to them, bearing their children, living in forests, and now even equating the silence of death with the vocabulary of silence of plant life. Like trees I wanted no more than I needed; I imagined my relationship with light as akin to that between it and trees; I tried to live to tree time, rejecting speed and excess. And yet I did not feel completely like a tree.

Not until a bird came and sat on my shoulder around sunset one day. I did not move. I do not know about the bird but I was certain that in the thinning margins of that forest in Baikunthapur I was, at last, ready to be a tree.

Sumana Roy

EPILOGUE

This is how stories have always ended in my mother tongue:

> Aamar kawthati furolo
> Notay gachhti murolo

> My story's come to an end
> The spinach leaves have folded,
> Its stem curled into a bend.

NOTES AND REFERENCES

PART I: A TREE GREW INSIDE MY HEAD

Tree Time

4   **Was it this that Salvador Dalí wanted to invoke:** One of Salvador Dalí's most recognizable works: *The Persistence of Memory*, 1931.

Women as Flowers

7   **In 'Ghumonto Puri', the second story of *Thakurmar Jhuli*, a collection of grandmother's tales in Bangla:** First compiled by Dakshinaranjan Mitra Majumder, *Thakurmar Jhuli* (Grandmother's Bag of Stories), 1907 (first published).

12   **'the one who commits himself will be as strong and straight as the oak or the ash':** Glenn W. Erickson, 'The Philosophy of Forestry', *Princípios*, 1998, pp. 95–114.

The Kindness of Plants

16   **'You can't write poems about trees when the woods are full of policemen':** Bertolt Brecht, *The Threepenny Opera*, Eric Bentley (ed.), Grove Press, 1964.

16   **'It has been said that trees are imperfect men':** John Muir, *John of the Mountains: The Unpublished Journals of John Muir*, originally written in July 1890, first published in 1938.

The Woman as Tree

17   **'The fig is a very secretive fruit':** D. H. Lawrence, *The Complete Poems of D. H. Lawrence*, Wordsworth editions, 1994.

18   **Suddenly, a different sort of person came up to it one day:** Banaphool, *What Really Happened: Stories*, Arunava Sinha (trans.), Penguin Books, 2010.

18   **'The reader encounters a vast, seemingly eclectic assemblage of Greek':** Annette Giesecke, *The Mythology of Plants: Botanical Lore from Ancient*

Greece and Rome, J. Paul Getty Museum, 2014.

19   'the one to drive love away, the other to cause it': Ibid.

19   'Scarcely did she finish her prayer when a heavy sluggishness overtook her limbs': Ibid.

20   'a flower bloomed there, the very colour of blood and like the flowers borne by the pomegranate': Ibid.

20   'Let him experience the same sort of love as I': Stephanie Paris, *Leveled Texts: Echo and Narcissus*, Teacher Created Materials, 2014.

21   'In its place they found a flower': Giesecke, *The Mythology of Plants*.

21   In the one collected by the poet and translator: A. K. Ramanujan, *A Flowering Tree and Other Oral Tales from India*, University of California Press, 1997.

21   'If you cut the smallest branch of a tree it is just as if you cut my finger': Ellison Banks Findly, *Plant Lives: Borderline Beings in Indian Traditions*, Motilal Banarsidass, 2008.

21   'As is a mighty tree so, indeed is a man': Ibid.

22   The root is the mouth: A. K. Ramanujan (ed. and trans.), *Speaking of Siva*, Penguin Books, 1973.

The Silence of Trees

26   'Knowing trees, I understand the meaning of patience': Hal Borland, *Countryman: A Summary of Belief*, Lippincott, 1965.

26   'The very concept of genre is as cold as the tomb': Andrei Tarkovsky and Kitty Hunter-Blair, *Sculpting in Time: Reflections on the Cinema*, University of Texas Press, 1987.

27   'I lean against a tree, I am a tree leaning': Margaret Atwood, *Surfacing*, Anchor Books, 1998.

PART II: I PAINT FLOWERS SO THEY WILL NOT DIE

Drawing Trees

36   'Not from the top downwards': Nandalal Bose, *Vision and Creation*, Nandalal Bose Birth Centenary Publication Series, K. G. Subramanyan (trans.), Visva-Bharati, 1999.

38   'The trunk is like the tree's backbone': Ibid.

39   'All those special arrangements to strengthen a branch at the joint!': Ibid.

Making Leaves

48   'There are only five leaves left now': O. Henry, 'The Last Leaf', *The Best Short Stories of O. Henry*, Random House, 2010.

48   'I've been a very foolish girl, Sue': Ibid.

89 'Pay attention to the garden': Ibid.

90 'How are the trees in Konark?': Ibid.

92 'I used to live in the cornermost house in Santiniketan's Uttarayan': Rabindranath Tagore, *Bonobani* in *Rabindra Rachnavali, Volume 8*, Visva-Bharati, 1986.

93 'This creeper must have a foreign name': Ibid.

93 'I am sending you a flower with this letter': Basu and Dutta, *Trees of Santiniketan*.

94 'This shall not be a garden of your favourite flowers': Ibid.

95 'Rathindranath Tagore knows flowers by his love for them and by science': *Silpi, Volume 1*, V. R. Chitra and T. N. Srinivasan (eds.), 1946.

Studying Nature

97 'We should strive to make the students familiar': *Prakriti Paath*, environment studies primer used at Patha Bhavan; see page 96.

97 In an essay on the education policy and ambition of the ashram in Santiniketan: Ibid.

99 'Oh you shaggy headed banyan tree': Tagore, *Rabindranath Tagore: Perspectives in Time*, Mary Lago and Ronald Warwick (eds.), Springer, 1989, p. 146.

99 One morning in the flower garden a blind girl came: *The English Writings of Rabindranath Tagore: Poems*, Sisir Kumar Das (ed.), Sahitya Akademi, 2004.

100 Supposing I became a champa flower: Ibid, p. 137.

PART V: I WANT TO DO WITH YOU WHAT SPRING DOES WITH THE CHERRY TREES

Having Sex with a Tree

107 'I want a boyfriend like a banyan tree': Sharanya Manivannan, *The High Priestess Never Marries: Stories of Love and Consequence*, HarperCollins India, 2016.

107 I swore never to starve again: Nitoo Das, 'At Age Eleven'. Accessed on 16 December 2016: northeastreview.wordpress.com.

109 A woman comes home to find that her boyfriend had turned into a tree: Adrienne Lang, 'The Tree', *The Gallery and Other Stories*, Senior Capstone Projects, Paper 291, 2014.

110 'If only my wife was like this tree, what happiness we would have': Mohinder Singh Randhawa, *The Cult of Trees and Tree-worship in Buddhist-Hindu Sculpture*, All India Fine Arts and Crafts Society, 1964.

Loving Trees

114 **'And the oak tree and the cypress grow not in each other's shadow':** Kahlil Gibran, 'On Marriage', *The Prophet*, Penguin Books, 2002.

116 **'It becomes almost a sexual ritual':** Ramanujan, *A Flowering Tree*.

PART VI: ONE TREE IS EQUAL TO TEN SONS

The Curious Botanist

126 **'the Laboratory merges imperceptibly into the gardens':** Das Gupta, *Science and Modern India: An Institutional History, c.1784-1947*, Pearson Education India, 2011, p. 978.

128 **'There is money in it—let me take out a patent for you':** *Indian Journal of History of Science, Volume 43*, Indian National Science Academy., 2008, p. 69.

128 **'The discoveries made will thus become public property':** Gupta, *Science and Modern India*, p. 978.

130 **'The secret of plant life was thus for the first time revealed':** Ibid, p. 980.

130 **'The remarkable performance of the Praying Palm Tree of Faridpore':** Sir Patrick Geddes, *The Life and Work of Sir Jagadis C. Bose*, Asian Educational Services, 1920.

131 **'A plant carefully protected under glass from outside shocks':** Gupta, *Science and Modern India*, p. 981.

131 **'Perhaps it was that sub-conscious impression':** Professor Jagdish Chandra Bose, *The Uphill Way*, speech delivered to the students at Presidency College, Calcutta. Accessed on 16 December 2016: http://resources.boseinst.ernet.in:8080/xmlui/bitstream/handle/123456789/74/CH-40-p.194-198-The-uphill-way.pdf?sequence=41.

131 **'whose pulsation goes on perpetually, like the human heart':** 'Automatism in Plant and Animal', *The Modern Review, Volume 3*, Ramananda Chatterjee (ed.), 1908.

131 **'One notices the same phenomenon in any healthy body':** Ibid, p. 382.

132 **'It is comparatively easy to make a rebellious child obey':** Ibid, p. 518.

132 **'Amongst plants, as with ourselves, there is, very early in the morning':** Ibid, p. 518.

132 **'In summer it takes *Mimosa* ten to fifteen minutes':** Ibid, p. 522.

133 **'In the script of the Morograph, or Deathrecorder':** Ibid, p. 525.

133 **'If the plant could have been made thus to keep its own diary':** Ibid, p. 519.

134 'Have plants never spoken?': Jagadish Bose, *Awbyaktoh*, Dey's Publishing, 2007.

134 'The seed is hiding below the soil': Ibid.

134 'Plants eat the way we eat': Ibid.

134 'Leaves have several tiny mouths': Ibid.

135 'The plant nurtures the seed with all its sap': Ibid.

135 There are so many countries and so many languages: Ibid.

135 'It's our good fortune that the plant script': Ibid.

135 The essay 'Nirbak Jeebon', The Silent Life: Ibid.

136 'A slight hurt causes only a slight disturbance': Ibid.

Gardens and Adultery

138 A little while ago, he has been given a packet of sketch pens: Satyajit Ray, 'Pikoo's Diary', *The Collected Short Stories*, Penguin Books, 2015.

140 To dub the plot of land that lay behind Bhupati's house a garden: Tagore, 'The Broken Nest', *Three Women*, Arunava Sinha (trans.), Penguin Books, 2010.

141 'had not had a child, had probably given up hope of having one': Ibid, 'The Two Sisters'.

141 'Now I know, as I'm about to die, that whatever else I may have achieved': Ibid.

142 'She had been banished from the very garden that had claimed her heart': Ibid, 'The Arbour'.

144 'Do you know the name of this flower?': Ibid.

PART VII: LOST IN THE FOREST

Lost in the Forest

151 'In the middle of the forest there's an unexpected clearing': Tomas Tranström er, *The Half-finished Heaven: The Best Poems of Tomas Tranström er*, Robert Bly (trans.), Graywolf Press, 2001.

152 'I will write something about the life in the jungle': *Indian Literature*, Vol 47, Issues 4-6, Sahitya Akademi, 2003.

156 'I lost my way one evening on the way back from a survey camp at Ajmabad': Bibhutibhushaṇa Bandyopadhyaya, *Aranyak*, Rimli Bhattacharya (trans.), Seagull Books, 2002.

156 Stand still. The trees ahead and bushes beside you: David Wagoner, 'Lost', *Traveling Light: Collected and New Poems*, University of Illinois Press, 1999, p. 10.

158 'Tell me, don't you mind living here all by yourself?': Bandyopadhyaya, *Aranyak*.

159 'the ideal state of mind which is properly the goal of every Krishna bhakta is also called Vrindavan': Charles R. Brooks, *The Hare Krishnas in India*, Motilal Banarsidass, 1992.

Wild Men and Lost Girls

164 'For two days I had the company of a girl': Yossi Ghinsberg, *Lost in the Jungle: A Harrowing True Story of Adventure and Survival*, Skyhorse Publishing, 2009.

164 'It was as though something of Jaipal's influence': Bandyopadhyaya, *Aranyak*.

164 'It is better for those who have to live within the strictures': Ibid.

165 'What if we think about ourselves as political plants?': Margarida Mendes in interview with Michael Marder, 'Plants Are the Perfect Self-Drawing Diagrams', *Los Angeles Review of Books*, 5 May 2015.

166 makes an important point behind the marginalization of plant life in our consciousness: Mathew Hall, *Plants as Persons: A Philosophical Botany*, SUNY Press, 2011.

167 'It was only here, in these lonely forests': Bandyopadhyaya, *Aranyak*, p. 32.

167 Unity dazzles on at least two counts: by its sum and by its division: Michel Serres, *Genesis*, Genevieve James and James Nielson (trans.), University of Michigan Press, 1995.

172 'Yet, I grieved, knowing that the forests of Narhabaihar would not stand for long': Bandyopadhyaya, *Aranyak*, p. 196.

173 'The shepherd went to fetch a small sack and poured out a heap of acorns on the table': Jean Giono, *The Man Who Planted Trees*, Shambala, 1999.

173 'he began thrusting his iron rod into the earth': Ibid.

173 'Creation seemed to come about in a sort of chain reaction': Ibid.

174 Payeng is Elzéard in real life: Rahi Gaikwad, 'The Man Who Grew Forests', *The Hindu*, 18 December 2015.

175 'This reserve is as long as the stretch from Paris to Switzerland': Ananya Borgohain, 'Son of the Soil', *The Pioneer*, 17 May 2015.

175 'The man was spending his own time and money': Ibid.

PART VIII: UNDER THE GREENWOOD TREE

Sitting Under a Tree

181 Under the almond tree, the happy lands: Lawrence, *Complete Poems*.

182 Under the greenwood tree: William Shakespeare, *Arden Shakespeare Complete Works*, Bloomsbury Publishing, 2014.

The Buddha and the Bodhi Tree

184 'The Bodhi Tree of the present Buddha, that is, Gotama Buddha':
Dipak Kumar Barua, *The Bodhi Tree and Mahabodhi Mahavira Temple at Buddha Gaya*, Bodhgaya Temple Management Committee, 2013.

186 The *Samantapasadika* brings to us today what reads like a history of violence: Buddhaghosa, *Samantapasadika: Buddhaghosa's Commentary on the Vinaya Piṭaka, Volume 1*, Pali Text Society, 1966.

188 'All about here (Lumbini) were Ashoka blossoms and in delight': B. D. Kyokai, *The Teaching of Buddha*, Sterling, 2006.

189 'Buddhaghosa mentions it was to the gandhakuti': John S. Strong, 'Gandhakuti: The Perfumed Chamber of the Buddha', *History of Religions 16/4*, 1977.

190 'this lofty perfumed house which is like unto a flight of steps to heaven': Barua, *The Bodhi Tree*.

190 'The lotus means the waters': *The Satapatha-Brahmana, Volume 2*, Atlantic Publishers.

191 In his book *Water in Culture*: Jayaratna Banda Disanayaka, *Water in Culture: The Sri Lankan Heritage*, Ministry of Environment and Parliamentary Affairs, 1992.

192 'whose fibres are patience, whose flowers are virtue': Barua, *The Bodhi Tree*.

193 'through envy, destroyed the convents and cut down the Bodhi Tree': Ibid.

194 Buchanan who visited the site in 1811 saw the tree in full vigour: Gunapala Piyasena Malalasekera (ed.), *Encyclopaedia of Buddhism*, Government of Ceylon, 1989.

195 'In the old sculptures the Buddha Himself is never represented directly': Thomas William Rhys Davids, *Buddhist India*, Motilal Banarsidass, 1903.

196 'The Buddha taught that everyone is a Buddha': Barua, *The Bodhi Tree*.

196 'It is wonderful, truly marvellous': Madhusudan Sakya, *Current Perspectives in Buddhism: A World Religion, Volume 1*, Cyber Tech Publications, 2011.

197 A Bhikkhu who enters the courtyard of a Bodhi tree: Karunaratne Gunapala Senadeera, *Buddhist Symbolism of Wish-fulfilment*, Sri Satguru Publications, 1992.

PART IX: THE TREE IS AN ETERNAL CORPSE

The Death of Trees

201 When great trees fall: Maya Angelou, 'When Great Trees Fall', *I Shall Not*

Be Moved: Poems, Random House, 1990.

211 **Tell me what you see vanishing and I will tell you who you are:** Stephen Taylor, *Oak: One Tree, Three Years, Fifty Paintings*, Princeton Architectural Press, 2011.

The Rebirth of Trees

214 **'Whatever food a man consumes in this world':** *Satapatha-Brahmana*.

214 **'As the result of evil karma, souls are born as plants':** Lance E. Nelson, *Purifying the Earthly Body of God: Religion and Ecology in Hindu India,* SUNY Press, 1998.

216 **The tales of transformation of humans into trees:** Ovid, *Metamorphoses*, David Raeburn (trans.), Penguin Books, 2004.

216 **The most recent among them is Robert Coover's story:** Robert Coover, 'The Crabapple Tree', *New Yorker*, 12 January 2015.

218 **'The Giving Tree' became 'Gachh Ma':** Narayan Sanyal, 'Gachh Ma'.

218 **the American poet and writer Shel Silverstein's 1964 illustrated story:** Shel Silverstein, *The Giving Tree*, HarperCollins, 1964.

How I Became a Tree

221 **'Leaving behind a tree definitely seems like a better option':** https://www.capsulamundi.it.

BIBLIOGRAPHY

Angelou, Maya, 'When Great Trees Fall', *I Shall Not Be Moved: Poems*, New York: Random House, 1990.

Atwood, Margaret, *Surfacing*, Anchor Books, 1998.

Banaphool, *What Really Happened: Stories*, Sinha, Arunava (trans.), New Delhi: Penguin Books, 2010.

Bandyopadhyaya, Bibhutibhushan, *Aranyak*, Bhattacharya, Rimli Bhattacharya (trans.), Kolkata: Seagull Books, 2002.

Barua, Dipak Kumar, *The Bodhi Tree and Mahabodhi Mahavira Temple at Buddha Gaya*, Bodh Gaya: Bodhgaya Temple Management Committee, 2013.

Basu, Satyendra Kumar, *Trees of Santiniketan*, Kolkata: Visva-Bharati, 1957.

Berkeley, George, *A Treatise Concerning the Principles of Human Knowledge*, New York: Dover Publications, 2003.

Bose, Jagadish Chandra, *Awbyaktoh*, Kolkata: Dey's Publishing, 2007.

———, *Rachana Samagra*, Kolkata: Dey's Publishing, 2013.

Bose, Nandalal, *Vision and Creation*, Nandalal Bose Birth Centenary Publication Series, Subramanyan, K. G. (trans.), Kolkata: Visva-Bharati, 1999.

Brooks, Charles R., *The Hare Krishnas in India*, New Delhi: Motilal Banarsidass, 1992.

De Botton, Alain, *The Pleasures and Sorrow of Work*, London: Vintage, 2010.

Deleuze, Gilles and Guattari, Félix, *A Thousand Plateaus: Capitalism and Schizophrenia*, Minneapolis: University of Minnesota Press, 1987.

Erickson, Glenn W., 'The Philosophy of Forestry', *Princípios 5 (6)*, Department of Philosophy, Ann Arbor: University of Michigan Press, 1998.

Findly, Ellison Banks, *Plant Lives: Borderline Beings in Indian Traditions*, New Delhi: Motilal Banarsidass, 2008.

Ghinsberg, Yossi, *Lost in the Jungle*, New York: Skyhorse Publishing, 2009.

Giesecke, Annette, *The Mythology of Plants: Botanical Lore from Ancient Greece and Rome*, Los Angeles: J. Paul Getty Museum, 2014.

Gibran, Kahlil, *The Prophet*, London: Penguin Books, 2002.

Giono, Jean, *The Man Who Planted Trees*, Boston: Shambala Publications, 1999.

Hall, Matthew, *Plants as Persons: A Philosophical Botany,* Albany: SUNY Press, 2011.

Henry, O., *The Best Short Stories of O. Henry,* New York: Random House, 2010.

Lawrence, D. H., *The Complete Poems of D. H. Lawrence,* Hertfordshire: Wordsworth Editions, 1994.

Lima, Manuel, *The Book of Trees: Visualizing Branches of Knowledge,* New Jersey: Princeton Architectural Press, 2014.

Malalasekera, G. P. (ed.) *Encyclopaedia of Buddhism,* Colombo: Government of Ceylon, 1961–2002.

Manivannan, Sharanya, *The High Priestess Never Marries: Stories of Love and Consequence,* New Delhi: HarperCollins, 2016.

Moon, Beth, *Ancient Trees: Portraits of Time,* New York: Abbeville Press Inc, 2014.

Nelson, Lance E., *Purifying the Earthly Body of God: Religion and Ecology in Hindu India,* Albany: SUNY Press, 1998.

Ovid, *Metamorphoses,* David Raeburn (trans.), London: Penguin Books, 2004.

Ramanujan, A. K., *A Flowering Tree and Other Oral Tales from India,* Berkeley: University of California Press, 1997.

Randhawa, Mohinder Singh, *The Cult of Trees and Tree-Worship in Buddhist-Hindu Sculpture,* All India Fine Arts and Crafts Society, 1964.

Ray, Satyajit, *Our Films, Their Films,* Hyderabad: Orient BlackSwan, 2001.

———, *The Collected Short Stories,* New Delhi: Penguin Books, 2015.

Senadeera, K. G., *Buddhist Symbolism of Wish Fulfilment,* New Delhi: Sri Satguru Publications, 1992.

Serres, Michel, *Genesis,* Genevieve James and James Nielson (trans.), Ann Arbor: University of Michigan Press, 1995.

Shakespeare, William, *Arden Shakespeare Complete Works,* London: Bloomsbury Publishing, 2014.

Sorenson, Roy, *Seeing Dark Things: The Philosophy of Shadows,* New York: Oxford University Press, 2011.

Strong, *History of Religions, Volume 16, No. 4,* May 1977.

Tagore, Rabindranath, *Three Women,* Arunava Sinha (trans.), New Delhi: Penguin Books, 2010.

———, *Red Oleanders: A Drama in One Act,* London: Macmillan, 1973.

———, *Rabindranath Tagore: Perspectives in Time,* Mary Lago and Ronald Warwick (eds.), Springer, 1989.

Taylor, Stephen, *Oak: One Three, Three Years, Fifty Paintings,* New Jersey: Princeton Architectural Press, 2011.

Tranströmer, Tomas, *The Half-Finished Heaven: The Best Poems of Tomas Tranströmer,* Robert Bly (trans.), Minneapolis: Graywolf Press, 2001.

Wagoner, David, *Traveling Light: Collected and New Poems,* Chicago: University of Illinois Press, 1999.